CW00471212

SOUL S⟨ ⟩⟨UE

SOUL SOURCE

58 INSIGHTS THAT TRANSFORMED MY LIFE

REGENIA MITCHUM RAWLINSON

Village Concepts Consultants

Published by Village Concepts Consultants

ISBN 978-1-5336-6529-4

Typesetting services by BOOKOW.COM

To my children David II, Bradford, and Brittany who taught me more about myself than I thought I needed to learn. My children also taught me how to recognize the important things in life. They are my inspiration and my joy. I am very proud of them.

To my husband who is my advocate and devoted

partner.

To my mother, Hazel Mitchum, who birthed

seventeen children and knows the value of the human spirit and how to uplift it and encourage it.

To my father, Solomon Mitchum (deceased), who

is missed each day for his wisdom, patience, and high expectations of all people.

PREFACE

In moments of solitude, I find communion with my inner-most being, my soul source. This connection also manifests amidst the bustle of a crowd, during a quiet walk, in the depths of meditation, or even in moments of idle reflection. It is in these varied encounters with my soul source that I am imbued with lessons and attain enlightenment. Often, this revelation is subtle, unfolding without grandeur. Yet, at times, it dazzles like a Fourth of July fireworks display, illuminating my life and patterns with sudden clarity. This light has unveiled countless issues, subjects, and situations previously obscured or only partially visible to me.

There have been philosophies, viewpoints, and beliefs I've encountered over the years that eluded my full comprehension. However, in the clarity provided by my soul source, their meanings become transparent. The adage that we enter this world with nothing and leave with nothing, leaving everything behind, never truly resonated with me until I delved deeper into communion with my soul source. It clarified that upon death, we indeed leave everything—our work, thoughts, and deeds, the tangible and intangible legacies of our existence.

Should one pass leaving a trail of deception and dishonorable actions, generations hence may find themselves defending, ex-cusing, or denying these deeds. Conversely, a legacy of respect and integrity opens doors for one's descendants, offering opportunities borne of a good name. My father, though financially poor at his death, bequeathed such a legacy. Known for his wisdom and trustworthiness, his name, Solomon, was held in high regard, despite personal flaws and actions that might have marred his legacy.

As I ponder my own mortality, I aspire to leave a legacy that ensures happiness and opportunities for my children, inspired by the understanding that a good name carries honor in life and benefits one's descendants in death. This book is a reflection on my conversations with my soul source, an exploration into insights that were beyond my reach without this profound connection. The insights shared here, gifted by my soul source, have enlightened me, and I offer them to you, hoping they might similarly illuminate your path.

Within these pages, you will discover 58 insights presented through sentences, paragraphs, lists, and dialogues. I do not seek your agreement or approval of these reflections, but I invite you to ponder them deeply. Your thoughts and feedback are of great interest to me, and I welcome your perspectives on what you read here.

Acknowledgments

I want to express my gratitude to my Soul Source. Thank you for the time and attention you lavish upon me. May I always remember that you are constantly present, accessible to me everywhere and at any time. My sincerest thanks.

"Practice Silience: It Can be Very Powerful"

CONTENTS

Introduction		1
1	I Am	3
2	I See	4
3	Facts And Truth	5
4	How Do You Become Something?	7
5	The Light	9
6	Desire	11
7	Understanding	12
8	Motivation And Belief	13
9	The Power Of Choice	14
10	Ownership	15
11	The Answer Is In The Problem	16
12	Lost	17
13	Repentance	18
14	Money	19
15	Life	21
16	Greater Truth	25

17	Reality	26
18	Peace	28
19	We Must All Give An Account	29
20	Freedom	31
21	Capture Your Energy And Make It Subject To You	33
22	Complaining	36
23	Speak Softly	38
24	If Your Eyes Offend You	40
25	Who Are You?	42
26	Demands	43
27	Owe No Man Nothing But Love	46
28	Loneliness	49
29	Freedom vs. Ownership	50
30	Relationship Or Oneness	53
31	Communication	57
32	Choosing	59
33	What Is Truth?	61
34	Rejection And Loss	68
35	Awake	72
36	Welfare God	74
37	God Is Not An Employer	79
38	Strait Is The Way	80
39	Suffering	81
40	Profit vs. Losing Your Soul	84

41	Let There Be	85
42	Seek	90
43	Love Thy Neighbor	92
44	Robbing God	94
45	Opposites	97
46	Faith	99
47	Everyone Is Looking For The Same Thing	104
48	Why Must There Always Be A Reason?	108
49	Being In Awe	111
50	A Gift	114
51	Justice	115
52	The Power Of Agreement	118
53	What Is Man Saved From?	129
54	What Does It Profit A Man?	131
55	Freedom and life	133
56	What Is Good	135
57	Faith And Love	137
58	Mathematics Answers Everything	139

INTRODUCTION

Frst, let me clarify what I mean by "Soul Source." The term "soul" refers to one's spirit, heart, psyche, conscience, and core being. "Source" denotes the origin or point of consultation we turn to when we seek deeper understanding, knowledge, or to satisfy curiosity about a subject or issue. The soul seeks, and the source provides. While we may have many sources of guidance, we often have a primary or "soul" source that we instinctively turn to first, akin to a default source. This Soul Source may evolve over time, yet the fundamental role of the Soul Source remains constant.

People identify their Soul Source in various ways. For some, it is the Great Spirit, Mother Earth, or close family members like parents, siblings, aunts, uncles, grandparents, or even a neighbor. Others find their Soul Source in religious texts like the Bible or the Quran, or in figures such as Buddha or Mohammad. Then there are those who turn to newspapers, magazines, therapists, psychologists, psychiatrists, astrologers, or palmists. My Soul Source is the all-knowing.

Some inherit their Soul Source from family teachings or ancestral traditions. Others discover theirs through reading, hearing about something or someone on the radio, TV, or social media, or through recommendations. The choice of a Soul Source is deeply personal, influenced by one's preferences, cultural background, and religious beliefs. My own Soul Source was determined by my upbringing in the church, cultural background, and personal exploration.

The Soul Source serves as a fountain of advice, comfort, assurance, information, planning, and guidance. It is sought after in both joy and despair—for expressing gratitude or seeking peace and solace. It assumes a leadership role in one's life, commanding respect, and reverence. Individuals defend and champion their Soul Source as it is integral to their sense of wellbeing and security, embedding deep-seated beliefs. Once committed to a Soul Source, a person aligns closely with their ideals and principles, which significantly influence their decisions and actions.

The Soul Source communicates in various forms—sometimes with a single word to prompt reflection, a sentence, a paragraph, or through entire books. It may also direct individuals to other sources for answers, and engaging in conversation with the Soul Source is entirely within the realm of possibility. The advice, guidance, information, comfort, and assurance received are sometimes referred to as revelations or epiphanies. My Soul Source has provided me with numerous insights, communicated through direct quotes, influences on my thoughts, and conversations.

This book is a collection of moments when I communed with my Soul Source and gained a deeper understanding than I could have achieved on my own. These insights, whether direct quotes, influences, or conversations, have enlightened me. I share them with you, hoping they will enrich your understanding as much as they have mine.

Insight 1

I AM

Soul Source: *You must first know who you are before you know who others are. You are what you say and what you see and what you believe. Affirm today who you are. See yourself as BEING these things, not being in possession of them.*

I am truth.

I am light.

I am wealth.

I am health.

I am sight.

I am wisdom.

I am courage.

I am understanding.

I am righteousness.

I am sanctification.

Insight 2

I SEE

SOUL Source: *To see is to be seen. It is only when you are seen that you are clear on what you see. You see through your own eyes. Therefore, you must see yourself clearly in order to see others and the world clearly. However, you see yourself is how you will interact with the world because your world is interpreted by you. If you see the world as a dismal place, you see yourself as hopeless. Others will agree with your assessment of yourself.*

If you want to change the way you see the world, change the way you see yourself. The world will bow to your image. If you see yourself as a leader, the world will honor this by providing opportunities for you to lead.

What are you? Declare it today.

Insight 3

FACTS AND TRUTH

SOUL **Source:** *Look at the facts but acknowledge the truth. The fact is you are angry; the truth is you are capable of love. The fact is you are sad; the truth is joy is within your reach of decision. The fact is you are arrogant; the truth is you are bold. The fact is you have evil thoughts; the truth is you can cast them down.*

Stop confusing facts with truth. They are two different things. Facts change. Truth does not. For example, a pine tree will forever be a pine tree. The fact is that a pine tree is three feet now, but it will grow if it lives. People have been confusing facts and truth all their lives. Do you know that the Bible is full of facts? Because you have considered the Bible a book of truths, you have deceived yourselves and others.

You shall know the truth and the truth shall make you free. Most of what you have learned in the Bible is fact and has nothing to do with truth. Anytime you decide what to do, separate facts from truth, and then act on truth.

Me: How can you know when you are dealing with truths or facts?

Soul Source: *Facts have the possibility and are highly probable that it will change; truth will not change.*

Me: When I try to come up with examples of truth, it is hard.

Soul Source: *That is because there are very few truths in this world.*

Me: What are they?

Soul Source: *Essence. Nature is truth but everything in nature is truth. The essence of nature is life. If nature loses life, the truth is it will die. Truth is significant. Truth is harsh. It has no feelings. Truth can be devastating or uplifting depending upon how you receive truth. Truth is boundless; without end or beginning. We look and there it is. Truth is ever increasing faith. Faith to believe in that which you believe. Truth has no shame. Truth has its own light. Who would light a candle and put it under the bed? Truth is consistent – you idiot! Can't you see that truth contradicts the things you hold as truth? If you hold something as truth and you find contradiction, it is not truth. Truth is timeless. Truth is perfection. Where you find truth, you find perfection. Even if you do not think so. Christ is the truth, and he was perfect. Truth is freedom. If you are involved in anything that causes you bondage, you are dealing with facts not truth.*

Insight 4

HOW DO YOU BECOME
SOMETHING?

SOUL **Source:** *Declare you are that which you desire to be, and it is so. That which you are, you will never want or desire to be because you are that which you desire. God is. He demonstrates that which he is. You can demonstrate that which you are. Whatever you bind on earth is bound in heaven. Whatever you loose on earth is loosed in heaven. Give thanks for that which you are.*

Me: Spirit, I thank you that I am. …Whatever

Soul Source: *You are that which you desire. You name it and it is so. Call those things to be as though they were. Clothes were given a name, and it was so. Shoes were given a name, and it was so. Animals were given names, and they were so. The heavens were given a name, and they were so. Man was given a name, and he was so. A house was given a name, and it was so. A car was given a name, and it was so. Jesus was given a name, and he is. God was given a name, and he is.*

Anything that you call by its name had the same shape and form before it was called by a name. The name gives a thing meaning and character. Name it and it shall be so. Calling a thing by a certain name will not change the thing but it will change the way you see it and what you believe it to be. If you call a couch a snake and believe it to be a snake, you will not sit on the couch because to you it has a different meaning and function. By your belief you shall be saved. Call a thing by any name you want to name it, and it will be whatever you name it. Not only will it be what you name it, but also it will function according to your definition of what it is.

Me: When I lived on the farm, we had a ditch in front of our house. At times in the year, if you look close enough, you could see crawfish. We would have never dreamed of eating those ugly looking things in that ditch. To my surprise about five years ago, I saw crayfish in the grocery store. We called them crawfish, but the supermarket called them crayfish. We did not think about using them for food, but the supermarket was selling them at what I thought was a high price. We thought of them as something to be avoided and scorned but the supermarket thought of them as a product to make money.

My husband grew up eating a thing called poke sally. It was a tall green plant with red berries and bright green leaves with red veins. It grew voluntarily so you did not have to plant it, but each year it would produce another crop. Where he grew up, it was considered a treat and something worth waiting for. We had the same plant in abundance where I grew up. We believed that the plant was poisonous and should not be eaten. Whatever you name a thing, it is that thing to you and will function as such.

Soul Source: *Declare and believe now that which you desire, and you are that which you declare and believe. It is impossible to behave like something you are not.*

Insight 5

THE LIGHT

SOUL **Source:** *When you can find the humor in life you are indeed on your way to learning how to use your sense of humor. The funny thing about life is that you will not get out of it alive. But if you find humor in it while you live, you will have life. Find humor in all that happens and know that "stuff happens" and there is not a thing you can do about it except make something happen yourself.*

Walk in the light and the light will find you wherever you are. When you have problems with the light, it is because you have not found the light switch. The world is full of light and there is a switch for every light. Once you find the right switch, the light will come on. It is automatic; it does not require thinking, procrastination, or planning. What you will need to seek is the switch. In most cases, the switch is in the same room or space you are in. Unless the light is controlled from a central place. In that case, go to the central place.

If it is light that you want, look in the place that you are in. The switch is that which brings you truth with or without pain. The light is the solace, the switch is the catalyst. The thing about light is that you can turn it on or off with the switch. But it takes you to do it. Once the light (truth) is on, you can see things in the room clearly.

Everything is what it is. A table is a table, a chair is a chair, and a bed is a bed. Whatever is there where the light comes on is there. Sometimes the furniture is in good shape and sometimes it has been abused or in bad shape. Life is likewise. When the light (truth) comes or whatever is there is there. Sometimes it is shabby and sometimes it has been taken care of because of its value. Whatever the case, find the switch and let there be light.

You find the truth by asking and seeking. When you enter a dark room, you use your hands to feel around to find the light switch. You often bump into objects; sometimes you even hurt yourself as you look for the light switch. Finding truth is the same. You must search, be willing to bump into things that may cause you pain, and never give up until you find truth. Truth is always in the same room or space that you are in. If you want to know the truth about who you are, ask the question and seek (pray) the answer. The truth to that question is in the same space as you are in.

Insight 6

DESIRE

Soul **Source:** *That which you desire will first be required of you. If you desire love, you must first give love. If you desire happiness, you must first bring joy into another's life. If you desire friends, you must first be friendly.*

Insight 7

UNDERSTANDING

ME: How can a man understand that which he does not understand?

Soul Source: *By understanding that which he understands. Understanding is to stand under that which you know. You move from place to place.*

Me: How can you move when you are standing?

Soul Source: *Standing only implies static in the physical realm. Standing in the spiritual realm is to stick to what you know to be true. Truth always attracts other truths. Therefore, you move from place to place. Confess and believe that which you know to be true and understanding of other things will come.*

Insight 8

Motivation And Belief

Soul Source: *Motivation and belief come by awakening. We must find and stir up the gift that is within us.*

Insight 9

THE POWER OF CHOICE

SOUL Source: *The power is in the choice. Whatever you choose, the power is in that which you choose to manifest it. If you choose to learn how to drive a car, the power to drive a car is in the choice to drive. If you decide not to learn how to drive, you will never drive. "As thou believe, be it unto you." Whatever you choose is what you believe you can do. "If you have faith as a mustard seed, you can remove mountains."*

Insight 10

OWNERSHIP

S OUL Source: *That which you seek to own, you will never pos-sess. Ownership implies an end. If you own something, others will not have free access to it. Heaven and earth were made for all.*

Insight 11

THE ANSWER IS IN THE
PROBLEM

SOUL **Source:** *The answer is always in the problem. Look inside the problem for the answer.*

Insight 12

LOST

Soul Source: *When one is lost, he constantly struggles to find his way home. One is lost if they are in the wrong vocation. One is lost when one is in a destructive relationship. One is lost when one is fearful. One is lost when one is envious. One is lost when anything one engages in causes pain and shame for himself or others. We all are lost in one way or another. We all are struggling to find our way home. Home to happiness. Home to complementary relationships. Home to love. Home to the right vocation. Home to freedom. Home to joy. When you are lost, you are fearful, hopeless, and lonely. Finding your way home is easy if you remember how, you got where you are and then do the opposite.*

Insight 13

REPENTANCE

SOUL **Source:** *Repentance means to change your mind about whatever. If you don't like the way you cook chicken, repent! Cook it another way. If you do not like the way you treat people, repent! Treat them differently. Repentance is a great spiritual truth and is a very practical application. The truth is, anything you change from the old way of doing things to a different or new way of doing it, you repent. Repenting is not just reserved, though it is most significant, for repenting of sin.*

MONEY

ME: What is the energy of money?

Soul Source: *The energy of money is death.*

Me: What do you mean?

Soul Source: *You see all things that are connected with money are in the state of decay.*

Me: What does that mean?

Soul Source: *Look for things which are decaying, and you have found the energy of money.*

Me: But all things decay and ultimately die.

Soul Source: *Yes, all things decay but do not ultimately die. Nothing dies but all things see death.*

Me: Aren't dying and death the same?

Soul Source*: No. Death means an end to that which you see in its present form. To die means that you never see it again. I tell* *you that the disciplines did not die, and you will see them again. The death of a thing gives rise to life of another thing. Do not be deceived. Money is made when one thing see death then money can be made at the beginning of each new life of a thing. If you want to make money, look for those things that are dying and give life to them in another form. That is why you see companies all the time redo and revamp their products and services; to give new life. Give life to death and money will come.*

Insight 15

LIFE

ME: What is life and what is life all about? I lament my dad's death. I am angry about my sister's life. I am wondering about what goes on in life. What in the hell life is all about?

Soul Source: *Life is hell. One who tries to save his life will lose it; one who loses his life will find it. Let it go and let another life be expressed through you.*

Me: What is that supposed to mean?

Soul Source: *Life is hell because you devote your whole energy to saving your life. That which you strive to save will eventually be lost. You cannot save life because there is no formula for preservation. Life continuously moves and changes. Life is a spirit; ask it what you will. Life is expansive and can never be contained. People get sick because they try to contain life. Sickness is life contained. Always give life free expression. If life wants to dance, let it dance through you. If life wants to sing, let it sing and clap, let it clap through you. If life wants to cry, let it cry through you. You do not have to live life but rather let life live through you.*

Your body is a mere vessel for all spirits to have expression. You choose the spirit that you want expressed through your body to the world. Remember legions? There is not one house; there are many spirits waiting for an opportunity to express themselves. Don't you see the power you have? They are some pawns in your hands. All is always available. Everything is a spirit. Life is not one thing but is unlimited. Life is a multiplicity of things. Don't be confused or sidetracked by looking at life as a single integrity. Life is anything that makes you alive. What is life to one is death to another?

Your big mistake is that you think life is the same for all. Why do you think some people love to dance and others hate it? Honor life in every person. What life is all about allowing what you find uplifting and divine to you to be expressed through your vessel and disallowing anything else?

At the point you allow anything that is not uplifting to you, you call death to be expressed and that my friend makes life hell. Hell is being in a state you are in and do not want to be but have chosen to be and you will not do anything about it. So slowly and painfully you experience death repeatedly again. Where the fire never dies!

The reason you allow such things is that you are afraid of losing something or someone. Only when you are willing to lose that you can truly live. If people only allow life to flow through them, they will live forever.

Me: What about living a holy life?

Soul Source: *Holy means to allow free expression of that which uplifts you and others. Anything else is not holy. If things bind you and restrict your freedom that is not life and that is not holy. Take off thou shoes for where you stand is holy ground!*

Me: What form of life?

Soul Source: *You are a free spirit. You must allow all that is free to be expressed through you. Ideas, writings, arts, conservatism, patriotism, politics, reader, singer, any talent, and any gift. If everyone leaves everyone alone, everyone would be fine. You all want others to live like you because you think you know the best way.*

Life is not what you make it. Life is what you allow to be expressed through you and that makes up your existence. Life is what it is. Life is the essence of existence. Existence is not the essence of life.

No one can make a life. All life is already made and perfect in its own right. It merely needs a vessel to express itself. Decide on the kind of life you want to allow and allow only those lives to be expressed. Life is not singular, and you live more than one life each day. Each emotion expressed is life.

Who you are is what you have decided to be expressed. It is a myth to think that you know who you are. Who you are is defined by the lives you allow and therefore who you are is subject to the life expressed at any given time. Who you are is fluid and dynamic. You can only know who you are by those lives that you allow to express themselves through you.

Who told you that you needed to be predictable and undynamic anyway? That is man's way of keeping you in line-stagnating your expression of lives. If you are stagnant, you will never experience the full range of lives and you slowly die of life deprivation.

If you never live again, you could experience every life in this moment and time. When they say life is too precious to waste, they are right. Each time you disallow life to express itself through your vessel, you have wasted life. It is not the life that is being expressed that is wasted but the life that is not being expressed. It is not the life of mediocrity that is being wasted but the life of greatness that is not expressed that is being wasted. That which is being lived (ex-pressed) is the highest or the lowest form of that which can be lived (expressed). Choose life. While everything is life, all that is not life to you is death.

Me: What in the hell is life all about?

Soul Source: *Choice of expression my dear, choice of expression!*

Choose the life you live!

Insight 16

Greater Truth

Soul **Source:** *Work towards a greater truth and the lesser truth will disappear*

Insight 17

REALITY

S OUL Source: *There is noise in silence. There is order in chaos. There are advantages in disadvantages. Look and see my little one, look and see.*

The same water that flows up comes down. Watch the waves to see how high they will go, yet they are brought down low. The creeks are full of fish but so is the ocean. Abundance is all around. Look and see my little one, look and see.

Walk a mile and you will see how the woods are thick and thin. Things are not always what they appear to be. Reality is in the midst. In the middle somewhere between right and wrong. Reality is only real to those who are in it.

Never be in reality. Find your way out quickly, then you will be where things are seen for what they are - in a dream in a forest - run and hide - dare not reality find you or you will die. Run and hide. Seek safety of the unreal the unimagined. Seek and you shall find. Knock and the door will be opened. Once you find that door, knock with all your spiritual knowledge. The door will open to a new world - run to that door - run, run, run.

Me: Where is that door?

Soul Source: *In every secret place. Where are the secret places? The secret place is where all the real stuff is hidden. You have many secret places. Many unopened doors. Unresolved issues of life are your secret places. A place where you hide all things that you do not want others to know about you.*

Insight 18

PEACE

ME: How can a man live a peaceful life?

Soul Source: *Be at peace with himself.*

Me: How does one be at peace with himself?

Soul Source: *By calling peace from all nations. Peace is found in all corners of the universe. Nations are those places in the universe where peace resides. When you have called peace from the nations, you can be at peace with yourself. Giving up noise and war within yourself is the price you pay for peace.*

WE MUST ALL GIVE AN ACCOUNT

ME: Taking a shower in the morning is always refresh-ing. Sometimes while in the shower through moments of meditation, wisdom comes to you in the most profound and simplest of forms. That voice that resonates within you brings you powerful and life-giving messages. This morning as I took my shower, my mind raced from one place to another and from one situation to another, the words came.

Soul Source: *You must answer the question why, somewhere and to someone at some time in your life.*

When truth comes, you will know it. It speaks to your heart and mind in a way that you cannot help but respond with gratefulness and awe. We all must be prepared to answer" why" for every action, every deed, and every thought we have had or will have in our life. It behooves us to choose carefully what we do and what we think. Whatever we choose to do, be prepared to answer the question "why." My hope is that your answer will be one that will magnify God, lift mankind to a higher level, and will allow you to look in the mirror and say, "you did it. Continue to be fruitful and multiply."

Insight 20

FREEDOM

Soul Source: *When you seek freedom, be sure that you seek it according to what will set you free. Never seek it according to what has set another free. For the things that have set another free, maybe the things that bring you into bondage or deepened the bondage that you already have.*

Whenever you go after freedom, determine what freedom is according to your standards and not the standards of anyone else. The recently divorced woman enjoyed her freedom because she was able to do the things she wanted to do; she had the financial resources. The married woman thought she would be able to do the same things, but she forgets that her situation was completely different. She failed to consider while the recently divorced woman gained her freedom, she became dependent on the one she had gained her freedom from.

Obtaining freedom at the expense of independence is no good. The slaves obtained freedom at the expense of independence. Once set free, they were still dependent upon the master to sustain them. The slaves had gained their freedom but were dependent still upon the ones they had gained their freedom from. The African American gained freedom from certain laws but remained dependent on the very ones that imposed those laws in the first place. Therefore, freedom without independence or at the expense of independence is no good. In fact, there is no freedom without independence. Seek freedom but covet independence!

Capture Your Energy And Make It Subject To You

Soul Source*: Each day our minds race to and fro, here and there, this place and that place. We find ourselves trying to follow and fulfill the desires of all of the energy out there in the universe.*

Capture all that imagination and bring it into captivity. All thoughts are energy drawing you into a place that it wants you to be. Thoughts are imagination until they are acted upon and then thoughts change and become a different energy form called action.

You will go after every imagination until you start controlling your energy field. Your imagination, your thoughts are your energy field. The breath and length of the energy field are determined by your constant following them. Energy is more powerful when it is concentrated and less powerful when it is spread over a large area. Every thought that you are able to capture and bring into your energy storehouse increases the power you will have to carry out the thoughts or imagination you want to put into action. But if you allow all your thoughts and imagination to run wild, you have little energy to carry out and fulfill your dreams. You will find yourself chasing a lot of thoughts, but soon run out of energy to pursue that thought and bring it to manifestation.

When you have a storehouse of energy, they can commune with one another and give advice to one another, when they are in the same place. "But a house divided cannot stand." Your energy divided cannot prosper and will serve only to frustrate your efforts and lessen your ability to get things done.

All imagination is not to be followed. Instead of following them,

you must capture them and bring them under your control so that you can decide how and when you will send them forth in the form of action.

A twenty-year-old young lady was gifted in many areas. She was gifted in music, art, sports, and academics. She worked very hard on each for a short period of time. She would spend hours on a piece of music to get it to a point to be presented to a record company. But it appears when she got to a certain point, her attention (thoughts, imagination) shifted to sports. She would give her undivided attention to sports while her academics and music were neglected. She would lose interest in sports and become more involved in her schoolwork, but by that time she was far behind, and it was hard for her to catch up. She became discouraged and wanting to accomplish something she turned back to a product that she was close to finishing– her music.

She would go from one energy field to another until she became frustrated. She lived a life of frustration until she reached the age of forty-five when it dawned on her that she had not accomplished much because she was allowing her thoughts to determine her action rather than her deciding what thoughts she would act upon.

You manifest your thoughts in the way and the time you want to manifest them. You allow your thoughts (imagination) to be in control, you will lead a life of frustration, anger, and disappointment. Capture your thoughts (imagination) and bring them under subjection.

Insight 22

COMPLAINING

Soul Source: *A feeling of being cheated or something being withheld from you that you think you deserve, often brings about murmuring and complaining. Murmuring and complaining leads to a sense of entitlement and a sense of entitlement leads to anger and counterproductive behaviors.*

For example, an employee feels that he gets little or no recognition for the long hours and hard work he does on the job. His willingness to stay late and perform duties that are not assigned to him goes unnoticed or seems to be expected. In time, the employee begins to feel that his employer is taking advantage of his willingness to stay extra hours and perform duties that are not part of his job description. His feelings of being taken advantage of lead him to start taking, in different forms, what he believes is due to him.

Instead of being early for work, he arrives at work just in time for him to begin his task. He stops working overtime and complains when someone asks him to stay late. He talks about his boss to his co-workers and tries to convince them how unfair and unappreciative the boss is to him. He stops volunteering to do additional tasks on the job.

Me: I understand better now why Jesus admonish us not to murmur and complain and do not be weary in well doing. When you become weary of the things you do because others seem not to appreciate it, you begin to murmur and complain. Jesus also assures that he will not forget our acts of kindness and love.

Soul Source*: Do not complain when people are not complementing you or giving you your just due, keep doing what you do and in time, what belongs to you will come. We often miss what belongs to us because we lose faith too soon.*

A classic example was the Israelites. They started murmuring and complaining about what they had to go through to get to the promised land. They delayed their accent to the promised land for forty years because of this. Do you do the same thing? What part of your life are you murmuring and complaining about? Stop it! If you are doing anything that you would consider "well," keep doing it.

Insight 23

SPEAK SOFTLY

ME: Winston Churchill coined the phrase "Speak softly and carry a big stick." I do not know about carrying a big stick, but what I have come to understand is that when you speak softly, people listen with anticipation and expectancy. It is though they think you have earth shattering news or something that has been kept from them.

Soul Source: *Human beings are big on secrets. Secrets are the business of the Secret Service and CIA. The secrets they guard are very important. If their secrets fall into the wrong hands, the consequences could be devastating. They speak in soft and low voices, or though it seems, and carry with them devices that would maintain their secrets even in a crowd. So, when they speak or talk of any of the secrets, they were charged with keeping, everyone sits up and takes note. So, it is with those who speak softly. People will take note of what they have to say. The challenge, if you decide to employ the "speak softly" philosophy is to make sure you have something to say that would keep the interest of the people. If you don't, speaking softly will work against you.*

People are intrigued if they think you have a secret and speaking softly will intrigue them. When you really want people to listen to what you have to say, speak softly and deliberately to the point of people having to concentrate to hear and understand what you are saying

Insight 24

IF YOUR EYES OFFEND YOU

ME: My daughter constantly complains about not being able to do what her friends do. Among other activities, she says they go to the movies after 9:00; have memberships at the YMCA and are able to go at will; and can take phone calls past 9:30. I guess I am not ready for my fourteen-year-old daughter to have the run of the YMCA or go to movies after 9:00 pm. This may be old fashion, but I call it prudence. After all, if she does all of this now, what will she have to look forward to in high school? Boys, maybe, but that is another story.

My sons complained of the same perceived injustices when they were at home. According to our children, we were, and still are, too overprotective and don't trust them to participate in some of the same activities in which their friends engage. My oldest son once told us that he was the only boy who had to be home before his date. Maybe his date should have an earlier curfew. 1:00 pm, in my opinion, is enough time to do anything you want to do that is within parental approval and less risky.

A few days ago, I went to the YMCA to enroll in swimming lessons. I finally got the nerves! After waiting fifteen minutes for the lessons to begin, a manager came out to tell me that the lessons were cancelled for the cycle I signed up for due to a lack of participants. They needed four to offer the lessons and I was the only one signed up. My husband and daughter were with me. I was disappointed because I wanted to learn how to manipulate the water before going to the beach in three weeks. It looked like that was not going to happen, disappointed, we started for the car.

On the way out of the YMCA, our daughter saw some of her friends coming into the YMCA and some leaving the YMCA. She remarked to me, "See everyone has a Y pass." We exchanged glance and continued to the parking lot. When we got in the car, we tried to engage her in conversation. Her answers were abrupt and with a tang of anger. Suddenly, a Soul Source moment.

Soul Source: *Don't let your eyes offend you, were the words. I was reminded of the scripture that says, "If your eyes offend you, pluck them out."*

Me: I wasn't ready nor was I prompted to tell my daughter to pluck her eyes out. But I was prompted to tell her since she feels that we do not allow her to do all the things her friends do, she gets angry because when she sees them, she wants to do the same things. I told her to appreciate what she has and the things she does enjoy, and then her eyes will not be so offended. When she sees others doing things, she will be grounded in the knowledge that she too has fun but in different ways. In time, she will do all that she wants to do, but for now, enjoy the things she gets to do. If she does not, she will lose the joy of the things at hand. Her eyes were offending her, and she needed to consider why.

Insight 25

WHO ARE YOU?

ME: I have come to realize that who you are determines how you get along with another person. Conflict between individuals is often caused by who they are rather than what they do. This maybe the answer to why the divorce rate is so how in the United States. The Bible warns us not to be unequally yoked. To be unequally yoked means that your personality is incompatible with your mates and that the two cannot be reconciled. To reconcile would mean that one person would agree to become what they are not and who they are not.

Soul Source: *Who you are is expressed by your attitude about things; what you like and dislike; what you like to do and what you do not like to do; and in your mannerism. It is impossible for anyone to give up who they are for a sustained period without becoming angry. A person can change what they do but never who they are. They can pretend for a time, but soon that will become too much of a burden for them to carry. Often that is what others want you to do – change who you are to be who they are.*

Insight 26

DEMANDS

Soul Source: *Which is worse, the demands of the needs of others or the seeker of those in need? I say both are equally fatal. Both kills from inside out. Both send you into a sphere of despair; some things you just want to hide from them all. Both are cruel in their never-ending demands to keep you stressed and in tears. Both make you feel that just one more time will be all you can take. Both prey on cowards. Cowards because they are afraid to tell others what is needed for them to be released from this bondage. Both are agony. Both seem to laugh at you when you get to that point.*

Be careful of how much you demand from others. Be aware of those who place demands on others. If you demand too much, you destroy the giver - just as Christ had to die for the demands and needs of others.

If you do not have someone who needs you enough, you wither and die. The one who needs dies because he cannot give. The giver dies to fulfill the needs of the one who needs them. Christ was the one who needed and the one who gave.

We must maintain balance. We must at times, be the one who needs and at other times be the one who gives. We must give as well as receive. That which you receive will be proportional to that which you give. That is why giving and receiving is so important. Although it is more blessed to give than receive, if you never receive you will eventually give to a point at which you have no more to give; and then you will begin to die.

Jesus had no one to give back to him; only in a few instances in the Bible you will find where he is the recipient of something from the hands of others. The vivid example is when Mary Magdalene poured the expensive oil on his feet and wiped it off with her hair. I can see why that special moment was recorded in the Bible. I am sure that Jesus was revitalized by her kindness and unselfish gift.

The garden was quite an ordeal for Jesus. He had given so much and still more was required of him. This must have been agony.

Rest is important. After a workday, you want to rest. It rejuvenates you. Just as God ordered that after seven years that the earth must rest, you must rest after a period of giving. During this time of rest also means you replenish your physical, emotional, and financial resources so that you will be able to give again after this period of rest.

For to love or to have a fruitful relationship with someone, reciprocity is the key. Otherwise, death is eminent of the one who gives and never receives. The giver always dies from the burden and the demands of others if she does not receive in kind. The one who needs always dies from the constant hurt and struggle for someone to give? Soon the pain and despair are so severe that they cannot survive.

Parents be careful how much you demand of your children. Keep it proportional to what you give to them. If you demand respect, give it. If you demand responsibility, be responsible to them.

Husband is proportionate.

Wife is proportionate.

Friend is proportionate.

Employer is proportionate.

If you have a need to be fulfilled by anyone, give that person something in return. This maintains and prolongs life. Never voice a need that you are not willing to give to someone yourself. Never give that which you are not willing to receive. What you sow, you will surely reap. Any viable relationship is giving and receiving.

OWE NO MAN NOTHING BUT LOVE

ME: The scriptures declare in John, "Owe no man nothing but love." Love one another as I have love you" "Be one as I and the Father is one."

Soul Source: *To owe no man anything is to completely be out of debt, both positive and negative with man.*

Owe no man an apology for to owe him an apologize means you have done something wrong to him.

Owe no man money. For to owe a man money is to be a slave to that person. If you are a slave, you cannot be at liberty to exercise your free will.

Owe no man kindness. For to owe him kindness means you have been unkind.

You only owe that which you have taken or borrowed.

Owe no man healing. For to owe her healing means you caused pain to her.

Owe no man happiness. For to owe man happiness means you have caused unhappiness.

Owe no man compliments. For to owe compliments means you have been critical.

Owe no man relief. For to owe relief means you have caused misery.

Owe no man obedience. For to owe him obedience means you have been disobedient.

If you do the thing, you will never owe the thing.

If you owe the thing, you do the opposite thing. When you stop doing the opposite thing, you don't owe the thing that causes the debt.

Owe no man forgiveness, for to owe forgiveness means you have judged.

Owe no man the truth. For to owe the truth means you have lied.

Owe no man respect. For to owe respect means you have been dis-respectful.

Owe no man peace and reconciliation. For to owe peace and recon-ciliation means you have been at war and in conflict.

Owe no man a gift. For to owe a gift means that you have with-holding a gift.

The only thing you owe man is love. You owe love because that is what you are supposed to be. If you are not what you supposed to be, you owe.

Owe no man honor. For to owe him honor means to have dishon-ored.

Mankind is in debt because he owes. If he owes, he will never be free.

Owe no man faith. For to owe faith means you have expressed doubt.

Owe no man goods. For to owe goods means you have stolen or cheated.

Owe no man obligation. For to be obligated is to be a slave.

Owe no man freedom. For to owe freedom means you have kept a man in bonds.

Owe no man nothing but love!

Insight 28

LONELINESS

Soul Source: *All that is in your life, you have laid claim to it. If peace is in your life, you have laid claim to peace. If happiness is in your life, you have laid claim to happiness. If unhappiness is in your life, you have laid claim to unhappiness.*

Be content with the moment.

Insight 29

FREEDOM VS. OWNERSHIP

SOUL **Source***: Moving something out of your life, the first step is to mentally let it go. You must release it to the universe if you have it in your life. You have not been willing to release it. Release it and begin anew.*

We do not release things because we are afraid that when we release it there will not be anything to replace it and if something is to replace it, we don't know what that will be. So, we feel at least we know that which we now have. The unknown is scary and uncertain. If you hold on to what is in your life, you will never know anything different.

Some things you want to hold on to because they bring you joy and happiness. Other things bring you pain, hurt, stress, frustration, but keep holding on to them just the same. If you hold on to those things, you hold on to the stress, pain, and frustration; it is a package deal.

When you hold on to things that do not serve you well, you live to regret it.

Some hold on to things because they do not want others to have them. Some hold on to people because they are afraid that they will desert them. People hold on to things or people because of fear, jealousy, greed, selfishness, to keep someone else from having them; it is pride.

If you ever come to the place where you can let go these things, you will also let go the motivation for keeping these things; and that my friend is freedom.

You must always live a life of detachment. That means you can at a moment notice release all that which binds you. All that captures you. Never consider yourself an owner of nothing but rather a steward. Knowing that one-day, that which you have today will someday be claimed by another. Enjoy it while it is in your care but be willing always to release it when someone else claims it. Be willing to release a person if the person wants to be released.

When you consider yourself to own something, you become a slave to that which you lay ownership. Ownership requires constant vigil to ensure that it stays yours. Ownership causes one to murder. Murder results when someone thinks what he or she lay claimed to be threatened and needed to be protected by him or her.

When you lay claim (ownership) to anything, you lose freedom to be who you are. You become a captive of what you say you own.

If you live a life of detachment, you will never have to worry about someone taking it away because it was never yours. You were only a steward of that which the universe asks you to care for a period.

Being the steward, I hope you helped it to grow. That is what stewardship means- you help it to grow for further use by the universe when it comes time for you to release it. Anything you have been given stewardship over and you somehow had a negative impact, you in fact owe the universe a debt that must be paid by you.

The universe is kind and forgiving. It will give you many opportunities to reprieve yourself. What the universe wants you to learn is that ownership brings heartache and sorrow and pain to all those you dare to lay claim to anything that belongs solely to the universe. That means everything belongs to everybody.

Walk upright before the Lord and he will bless you with all manner of blessings.

Seek blessings not ownership. Learn the meaning of stewardship and you will never want to be an owner again.

Even, I, The Lord, do not own. But rather, I have made all that I have made for mankind to enjoy. I won't even claim it to be mine and neither can mankind claim it to be his. It belongs to no one.

Free yourself. Stay away from ownership. Live a detached life and live a life of joy, peace, and contentment in the Holy Ghost. Amen. I have spoken it.

Insight 30

Relationship Or Oneness

Sᴏᴜʟ Source: *You have been fooled for a long time that the way of the world is the way of the world. What is the way of the world? The way of the world is destruction. Anything that decays is the way of the world. The world cannot offer anything of lasting value. The way of the world is constant flux and change. It carries you to high mountains and brings you down to the low peaks. There is nothing to be desired about the way of the world. Look around you and see all the things which are new today but old tomorrow. Things that are alive today and dead tomorrow. The way of the world is destruction.*

Your life is part of the way of the world. All things in your life change and decay. Relationships change and often decay. Relationships with one another are the way of the world.

Relationships and oneness are different. Being one means being one. There is no second party. Relationship means two or more. It means separation. If you see yourself in a relationship or separate from another person, there will be decay and conflict and change.

It is only when you see yourself as one, can you treat others as you would have them treat you.

I never said I wanted a relationship with you. I said I wanted to be one with you.

Oneness is a term that seems difficult to understand yet quite simple. Oneness is a journey into wholeness with yourself. You must integrate all parts of yourself. The reason you talk about relationships and not oneness is because you are separate from yourself. So, you have all these parts or pieces of you that need to become you. You are everything. You are all of you. All the parts and pieces are you.

Me: You just said I had to integrate.

Soul Source: *Integrate does not mean to remove or separate. Integrating means to accept all and learn all and know all. When you integrate something, you put it all in the one. All the pieces and parts operate as one.*

Me: Does that mean I accept the good and bad about me?

Soul Source: *Which part of you is good? Which part of you is bad? When I made you, I said, "You were very good!" Who judged you to be otherwise?*

The world is constantly trying to have a relationship when I have called you into oneness. Relationship because it consists of two or more separate integers, will decay.

Customers change banks because they do not like the relationship anymore. Divorce occurs because the relationship changes. If you are one, you can never leave yourself.

Oneness means you are whoever or whatever you have given yourself to. Therefore, it is not a relationship but oneness. Change your mind. Repent of this error. Talk only about oneness and not relationships.

Oneness is not a command, but it is a road to peace. Jesus prayed for oneness, but he never commanded it. He commanded that you love one another. Love is everywhere in the universe. Love is the universe's glue. It holds everything together. Once you become one, there is no need for love because you are love. You become that glue that holds other things together. Until you become one, you must have love to help you build positive relationships.

You look at alone as being by yourself. Being alone simply means that there is no interference from others, and you are free to enjoy your oneness with all.

Me: God help me to fully understand and accept your word. Teach me all things. Thank You!!!!!

Soul Source: *With parents and children, the struggle is not in developing a relationship; the struggle is in desiring to be one. They can never be one in a master/slave relationship. They must agree to be one. The struggle is usually in destroying the relationship. Both see themselves as separate from one another and they both fight against this separatism. Oneness means openness, freedom, and safety with another person. Relationship always means you only share part, and you hide things. That is why the parent and the child complain of a lack of understanding of each other. Oneness agrees. A relationship has no agreement but rather is transitory. Oneness never changes. Oneness gets rid of barriers and shut the mouths of loins.*

You become one when you receive the essence of another. You receive the essence of one another by constant revelation of yourself. Only you can reveal yourself to another. Without revelation of yourself to another, you can never be one with another. Jesus said, "I do what I see my Father do." "I speak what my Father tells me to speak." The Father revealed himself to the Son and the Son kept nothing from the Father- not even his agony.

God said that he spoke with Moses mouth to mouth. That means he was one with Moses. He revealed himself to Moses and he knew Moses well. If you want to be one with God, you must allow him to reveal himself to you and you must be willing to reveal yourself to God. Not that God don't already know you, but he desires that you talk with him about you. Through your communion with God, you will learn of him, and he will teach you of yourself. Then you will be able to reveal your true self to others so that you can be one with others. Revelation is the key to oneness.

Oneness also means you are willing to let the will of others be done for the sake of others. Jesus said, "Not my will but thine will be done." The Holy Spirit gives you the courage to become one.

Insight 31

COMMUNICATION

ME: How to communicate effectively with one another has been studied for centuries. Ever since the event that took place at the tower of Babel, man has had difficulty in communicating with each other. Man has trouble understanding each other. Why is it so hard to communicate?

Soul Source: *Communication occurs when we give to the other. When we care about what the other person cares about, communication takes place. At the tower of Babel, the people had several things going for them 1) they talked the same language 2) there was an agreement about what each word meant 3) they had a common goal 4) they all wanted the same thing 5) they were at peace with one another 6) and they trusted one another. All were willing to give to one another and all were willing to receive from one another. Giving and receiving are the cornerstones of communication. It is impossible to communicate with someone else if you are unable or unwilling to give that person what he or she needs to receive from you. For example, some people need to feel emotionally safe before they can either give or receive support, advice, or guidance. In other words, that person would have to trust you with* *his feelings. Feelings are the most fragile thing to entrust someone else with. Therefore, he must be sure that his feelings will not be battered or abused.*

Communication is more of an art than a science. It is not something to be studied and then experiment with. Rather it is something that is constantly changing and unfolding with the individual. It is not precise. We cannot measure or tabulate it. The people define communication involved. To communicate, you have to know who you are in an exchange with, what that person values, and what is necessary for you to develop a connection. Once they develop a connection, then you can give and receive and vice versa.

The only rules of communication are the rules set by you and the person with whom you are in fellowship. Communication does not happen at the physical level. Communication occurs at the deepest recesses of the soul. Communication happens when there is a mutual understanding that individuals involved can participate in some sort of exchange at a certain level.

Communication does not take place at the same level with all people. It takes place whenever the individual defines. A mother communicates with her child on a different level than she communicates with a niece or nephew. The deeper the level of communication, the more gratifying the fellowship. Fellowship is the first step to developing a relationship. If you want a deep relationship with someone, focus more on fellowship.

Insight 32

CHOOSING

SOUL **Source:** *God never asks you to choose between two people, he asks that you choose between him and others. "There is no man that has left house, or parents, or brethren, or wife, or children, for the Kingdom's sake who shall not receive manifold in this present time, and in the world to come life everlasting." He never tells a wife to choose between her mother and her husband. He never tells a husband to choose between his brother and his Father. He tells everyone simply to choose him. Sometimes by choosing God, others will be offended if the chose contradicts what they believe. It may appear to them as though your choice to follow God also puts you on the side of the person they object to or verse versa.*

Me: So, if the husband thinks you should stop communicating with your family and if he tells you that either you stop talking to them or he will leave, this is not of God. If a friend tells you that you cannot be friends with someone she does not like and if you continue to be friends with this person, you cannot be her friend, this is not what God requires. If you are ever pressured into choosing between two people, this is not of God. Choose God and the rest will take care of itself.

Soul Source: *Just know that by choosing to follow God, your loved ones or friends may get offended and begin to persecute you. Do good to them also.*

Insight 33

WHAT IS TRUTH?

SOUL **Source:** *For you prophesy in part. Tell them that they know and understand in part. That the other part that they do not know have been hidden from them for ages until such time I deemed it necessary to unveil greater truths. The truth has always been there but hidden from them. They have been blind but now they see; lost but now they are found.*

All that is, will be a-gain. All that is to come will come a-gain. All that breathe the breath of life will live a-gain. They that die will die a-gain. The word a-gain means no matter what you do, you will see a-gain.

Me: What do you mean?

Soul Source: *I mean that everything in your life, everything in your death, is gain unto you. Because everything in your life and everything in your death is a reoccurrence of something before only this time it is better for you. It is a-gain. That is why little children will ask you to do something that is pleasurable to them a-gain. Because they gain something each time you do it. You are doing* *what you are doing now because you are gaining something by doing or saying or being it.*

Me: Why don't I feel like I am gaining something? Why do I feel miserable sometimes?

Soul Source*: Because you only see partly and darkly. You do not understand the basic principle of light and darkness.*

Me: What is the basic principle of darkness?

Soul Source*: Light hides the darkness, but darkness can never hide the light. When you are seeing darkly, you cannot see the whole of light.*

Me: How do you see the whole of light?

Soul Source: *See truth.*

Me: What is truth?

Soul Source: *Truth is where you find it.*

Me: I do not understand what you mean by that.

Soul Source: *The truth, my child is that which brings the light into your life. When truth comes, darkness will flee. When truth is not around, darkness is there.*

Me: What are you saying about seeing in part?

Soul Source: *That you must search for the truth (light), and then you will know the truth and the truth will make you free.*

The truth is everything in your life that is a-gain. A-gain has two meanings– to occur more than once and you are blessed when it occurs.

Me: Some people won't believe this. How do I convince them?

Soul Source: *Just tell them and they will understand what you and me are saying.*

Me: How do I put this in a sermon or message?

Soul Source: *A sermon is not necessary. Write it out, distribute and discuss.*

Me: That is different from how we deliver a message.

Soul Source*: That is the problem, too much modeling and not enough creativity.*

Me: What is wrong with modeling?

Soul Source: *Nothing, as long as you model something you have never seen before. Model the unseen.*

Me: How do I do that?

Soul Source: *Listen, my child, listen.*

Me: Why does it have to keep coming a-gain?

Soul Source: *If it does not, you will never evolve into greater and greater truth. Truth is revolution. Truth is spiral. Truth is circular. Truth is not on a continuum. You will not find truth in a straight line.*

Me: What is this thing about going from glory to glory?

Soul Source: Who told you that?

Me: You did. The Bible did.

Soul Source: *That is correct, the Bible and the Bible are not I.*

Me: But you inspired the words in the Bible.

Soul Source: *This is truth. There is no word that is uninspired. But I do not necessarily inspire the meaning or the context in which the word is used. But rather by those who write from their point of reference and time. There are not layers of glory; it is only one glory but different degrees of that glory.*

Soul Source: *There is only truth, different degrees of truth. If I am truth and I am everything* and *made everything, everything is truth.*

Me: What about lies, I thought that there are opposites in this universe?

Soul Source: *Even the opposites are different degrees of the same truth.*

Me: What about heaven and hell, they are opposites?

Soul Source: *No, they are not. Remember truth is spiral and circular. It goes up and down and around and around. So is heaven and hell. It is the experience within the spiral or circle that defines your state of being at any given moment.*

Think about the universe. There is nothing straight. Nothing on a continuum. Everything is circular, spiral, or revolving. Circular, spiral, and revolving causes evolution. In other words, it causes change because everything is in constant motion.

Just as there will be day a-gain, you go from experience to experience and each time you will make a-gain. Just as with each day, you get older, you get more knowledge and yet your days may go along pretty much the same each time.

When you look for truth, look for it in each experience. Truth revolves. Let me put it this way, truth is a pattern not a process.

Me: What do you mean?

Soul Source: *I mean truth makes patterns. When you are looking for truth, look for a pattern. The pattern or path one chooses each time is truth for that person. Truth is not a process because a process says there are steps or certain things must happen. When you want truth, look for a pattern.*

You must get the idea out of your head that there is a way to express truth or a way to do truth. Truth is not a recipe - a dash of this and a pinch of that. Truth is where you find it - in a pattern. Creation is that truth. A spiritual law is the truth. Trees are the truth. Each type of tree has its own pattern. Birds are the truth. Each type has its own pattern. Humans are the truth. Each human feels and acts the same way under similar circumstances.

There is no such thing as lies. Everything is an expression of truth to some degree. Everything has a pattern. Even when something does not have a pattern, the pattern is that it does not have a pattern.

Me: What about things that destroy lives? Are they truth?

Soul Source: *Do they have a pattern?*

Me: Yes. Alcoholics have a pattern. Abusers have a pattern. Workaholics have a pattern.

Soul Source: *Then they are truths.*

Soul Source: *People make mistakes when they tell others that they lie or live a life of lies and deception.*

Me: But the Bible talks about self-deception.

Soul Source: *When the Bible talks about self-deception, what I meant was that people deceive themselves when they think they are deceiving others. Others can easily see how you are expressing or experiencing truth, but you try to fool others. For example, hiding alcohol. Come on! Do you not think others know? The only reason to hide something or you do not want others to know what you are doing is because you are not comfortable with the truth you are expressing.*

Truth brings light and sometimes that light blinds for a while. It startles you until you adjust. Once you have adjusted, you wondered what you did before you had the light. But if you are not careful; the truth that gave you light is the same truth that could bring you blindness. Remember truth continues to revolve, it is not static. If you see truth as static and final, it will eventually blind you a-gain. But even in that blindness you will a-gain grow. Once you see the truth a-gain, know that this is only a degree of truth, and that truth constantly evolves and therefore has unlimited degrees. The only way to remain in the light is to go where truth goes. It will never take you anywhere darkness resides.

Truth begets truth. When you see truth (light) know that this is a degree of truth.

Me: Many people would say that Jesus was the truth.

Soul Source: *They are correct. But Jesus was truth expressed in a high degree but not the highest truth.*

Me: What is truth expressed in the highest degree?

Soul Source: *I do not know. I have never seen it nor will you. There is no end. Glory to glory is from one degree to another. But not a destination. Not a final stopping place. You will never arrive. So, enjoy your experiences.*

Me: Truth speaks of **existence** - reality or illusion.

Soul Source: *Truth never changes.*

Truth does not define.

Truth does not validate.

Truth does not make judgment between good and bad; right or wrong.

Truth points to results and is not concerned with placing a value on those results.

Truth will make you free.

Truth has no preference.

Truth has no emotions.

Truth is everywhere.

Truth does not assign labels.

Truth points to results. It is the effect of cause.

Truth occurs at a time and place where knowledge and understanding come together or intersects.

REJECTION AND LOSS

SOUL Source: *Everything you have ever denied that came to you, but you really wanted it, is part of your self-conscious mind. If you really want to know what is in your self-conscious mind, look at the things that were pleasant things you wanted, but rejected because of the opinions of others. The key word or shall I say, the key period to the self-conscious mind is rejection.*

Soul Source*: That thing that you consider a loss automatically plays out in your life constantly.*

Me: What do you mean by loss?

Soul Source*: Loss as in generosity and reciprocity.*

Me: I don't understand.

Soul Source: *These two words are twins. They must occur at the same time for fulfillment to take place.*

Me: What does this have to do with rejection?

Soul Source: *If the two do not occur at the same time, you feel rejected. If you give someone something, anything (generosity) and* *that person does not accept it (reciprocity) you feel rejected. If someone gives you something and you do not accept it, the person feels rejected. In either case, rejection takes place and is stored in the self-conscious mind. The self-conscious mind automatically, at every opportunity, reminds you by transmitting a feeling of uneasiness, unacceptance, guilt, and unworthiness that you must not be generous or receive generosity in each and every situation.*

Those times when your self-conscious mind transmits feelings of acceptance, worthiness, gratefulness, and peace, it signals that it is ok for you to be generous or receive generosity.

To revamp or cleanse your self-conscious and make it congruent with your conscious, do not reject generosity and give generosity under all circumstances. Be conscious of the feelings generated by all situations. When you are feeling unworthy, accept. When you are feeling rejected, give. You identify rejection by your feelings. Any feelings of inadequacy speak of rejection. Any feeling of completeness and peace speaks of generosity and generosity equals acceptance.

If you want to revamp or cleanse your subconscious mind, look for rejection and generosity. Reject nothing. To reject manes to withhold something of yourself and to withhold something from others.

Soul Source: *Your subconscious mind is racked with pain because you have rejected. And so, your life is filled with rejection. God is not mocked, as a man soweth, he also reaps.*

You also tend to make people wait because you have always had to wait. It seems, as your life is a great big promise unfulfilled most of the time. But filled with unrewarded hard work. Give people what they want when they ask if possible. Stop making people wait. Stop living your life in the future and the future will be now. Remember there is no such thing as the future. The now is all you have. Even when tomorrow comes, it will be too late for this moment.

Waiting to give or receive is a sin. One of the greatest sins. To wait means that you reject the moment. If you reject the moment, the moment will reject you. But not just this moment, every moment. Because each moment happens all at once. One moment is no different from another in time – so if you reject in one moment, the subconscious will transmit or transfer that rejection to all moments pertaining to like or similar situations. If you were generous in one moment, the subconscious will transfer or transmit all generosity to all similar moments. To the subconscious all similar or related moments are the same.

For example, if you give to a person in need and generate a good feeling. The next time an opportunity to give comes up; you will feel good about giving. If on the other hand, you feel angry about giving, each time the opportunity to give comes up; you will feel angry and will not give. You have rejected. And so, it will be in every similar or related situation until you change your feelings about giving in those situations. The only way to change is to do the opposite. Follow after peace. That is doing the things that cause you to experience peace. Peace is about who you want to be. Another example, if you desire to tell your loved ones about your feelings of your love, you reject that moment in time, and when similar situations arrive, you will experience shyness, inhibition, sadness, and nervousness. They will occur each time until you do the opposite each and every time.

The reason people reject is for protection. The reason people are generous is for the soul. Rejection is about preserving the illusion of this world. Generosity is about bringing heaven here on earth.

Your attitude toward money has been lack. $500,000 is a lot of money and deep down you did not feel worthy of that money under the circumstances you think you have to work mega hours. In fact, what you have to impart to teachers is worth much more than what you are asking. Stop rejecting expensive things. All of it goes hand and hand. You are worth every penny because they are worth every penny. Stop justifying. Yes, what you say is true. They are worth every penny, but even if they were not, you still are.

AWAKE

SOUL **Source:** *Our job is to awaken people from sleep. Rest and sleep are two different things. Sleep does not necessarily mean rest. Even when the mass of men is asleep. They are at the same time restless. Only when they are awakened can they have peace with themselves and peace with God. God requires a restless nation to be awakening to the full potential within. He has placed treasures in the body and yet they do not see nor understand how the treasures are used or what they were given for.*

Awaken the nation to its true purpose and true nature. They are not sent to sleep a sleep of disease. Their sleep is a disease to the things of God. Their sleep produces little foxes and prevents that which is there to produce to the highest. When you are awakened, you will see the light. The light is in the awakening of the soul and the spirit of man. The way to awakening is found in the tunnel of thoughts. Thoughts that are buried deep in a dark cave. The cave is cold as ice and causes the plans to be thwarted by the lack of watchfulness and wakefulness by the carrier of thought.

The carrier of thought is everything that surrounds one. When one is surrounded by thoughts, one must be reminded of the source from which it comes. For thought comes from many sources; sources you do not have knowledge of nor understand. The thoughts you now have are not your thoughts. The thoughts you now have are only a far cry for the thoughts waiting to be produced in your tunnel of thoughts frozen in the cave. Your thoughts are asleep deep within and must be awakened by a new source. That new source is I. For I am the flames that melt the ice. I Am

WELFARE GOD

ME: I can't believe I am in the shower getting ready to begin another school year." "What happened- I prayed and prayed."

Did God not hear my prayers, or did he not understand what I was asking for?

Maybe I did not pray the right way.

Maybe I was not holy enough for him to answer my prayers.

Well, I guess I have a lot of cleaning up to do before he answers me.

But the Bible says, "Ask and I did." "I really don't understand what else I am supposed to do.

I thought God was a merciful God.

I knew he saw me crying many, many times because I did not want to return to the classroom.

Why is he making me go back?

Well, I guess that is what he wants for me at this time in my life.

But I don't understand why he wants me to be unhappy when he promised me joy.

Is there any benefit to serving a God like this?

I guess my faith was not strong enough.

As I pondered these questions in the shower, a still small voice responded,

Soul Source: *God is not a welfare God.*

Me: God is not a welfare God, what did this mean? I asked. No response.

So, I dried my body, got dressed, dressed, and fed my children, and off we went to school for another year.

Me: Over the course of the next few months, I would come to understand the meaning of "God is not a welfare God." I started gaining some insight when I read, "faith without works is dead." So, it had nothing to do with my faith or with God love, mercy, or grace. But it did have something to do with the fact that I did not act in that faith by doing something about my own situation. I was praying, but nothing else. What I have come to realize is that in the absence of action, there is no faith. I did not look for alternatives to going back to the classroom. I guess I had a welfare mentality. The problem was with me rather than with God.

What is the welfare mentality? I wanted something for nothing. Advantage, benefit, gain, profit, prosperity, happiness, relief, charity, and assistance are some of the words used to describe welfare. I desired all these things but wanted them given to me by someone I thought could and would simply if I asked. As I thought about the Bible and some of the things that God promised his people, I came to understand that all of his promises required some action on the part of his people for these things to manifest in their lives. For example, when he pledged the promise land to the Israelites, he told them that they would have to go in and possess it. In other words, they had to do something. Even regarding salvation, a person has to accept Jesus into the heart to receive salvation.

The welfare mentality has caused the death of many dreams, the destruction of relationships, and encouraged a cycle of poverty. The only way to rid yourself of such a destructive mentality is first to recognize that the welfare mentality exists. In the absence of this recognition, taking the second step would be impossible. The second step is to examine your own thought processes and determine if you are plagued with the welfare mentality. To determine if you have this mentality, ask yourself the following questions:

- Do I usually try to figure out how to get something for less or without paying anything?

- Do I look for opportunities to give or do I usually seek occasions to take? Giving does not always have to be material things. Sometime just a kind word is a huge gift.

- Do I always buy the cheapest food and clothing? Buying the cheapest clothing and food is different from looking for the best deal or shopping for the best product at the best price.

- Do I want the "Good Life" but not willing to do what it takes to have it?

- Am I angry and jealous of people who seem to have it all?

- Do I believe that I must save for a "Rainey Day?" This question looks directly at motive. If you are saving for a "Rainey Day" out of fear of future lack, you are in trouble. Remember, that which you fear tends to come upon you. But if you are saving because you desire to be fruitful and multiply that which you must help your family and others, you are on the right track.

- Do I try to solve my own problems, or do I generally depend on others to find solutions for me?

- Do I take responsibility for what happens in my life, or do I blame others most of the time?

- Do I spend most of my time thinking about my needs being met? When you spend most of your time thinking about your needs, you are concern about sufficient resources and you question if God or others can supply your needs.

- Do you spend a lot of time daydreaming and less time doing what it takes to make your dreams come true?

These ten questions are not all inclusive, but they will help you to ponder your own state of mind. The third step is to do something about it. Doing something is as simple as doing the opposite of what you are doing now. For example, if you seek opportunities to take, start looking for ways to give.

Soul Source: *The welfare mentality is a thief that comes to kill a valuable harvest, steal potential, and destroy dreams and lives.*

Insight 37

GOD IS NOT AN EMPLOYER

S OUL **Source:** *Is God an employer? No! God has sent us to do the same work that he has done. He has sent us to heal the sick, give sight to the blind, set the captives free, make the lame walk, preach the gospel to the poor, heal the broken-hearted, and to set at liberty those that are bruised. He did not tell us to work for him. If we worked for God, he would be an employer. We are joint heirs with Jesus. Jesus came to do the work of his Father and so must we.*

Insight 38

STRAIT IS THE WAY

S OUL Source: *"Strait is the way and narrow is the gate."* What-ever you hold me to, you must do yourself. That is how you are going to be judged. Hold others to that which you can and will hold yourself also.

Insight 39

Suffering

Soul Source: *When you allow sin to control your life, you will suffer and be in bondage to that which is in control. The greatest suffering occurred on the cross because all sin of the world was poured upon Jesus Christ.*

The stripes were the result of fear and envy. Fear and envy will scare you. Disease or foreign matter in your body causes sickness. If none exist in your body, you would not be sick. Sin is a disease or foreign matter that invades your body. Get rid of the foreign matter and you get rid of the sickness that it causes. All sin will scare and render you in a diseased state.

To the extent that you are willing to let go of sin, is the extent to which you are free. You are free from suffering when you let go of the sin in your life. Suffering is not about denying yourself a good life with wonderful friends and having a good time. Suffering and denying yourself is about being willing to do the thing that is pleasing in God's sight. It is suffering because your opposite wants you to do otherwise. Your opposite would have you trash someone's name when God says that slander is not godly. Your opposite will tell you to steal another's property, when God tells you that "Thou shalt not steal." Suffering and denying yourself is to choose the higher thought. If you do this, "you shall reap what you sow."

You suffer because you have greed, hate, strife, contentions, envy, jealousy, and a host of other things in your life that produces death in one way or another. If you are suffering, you are not suffering because you are denying yourself a good time. You are not suffering because you are denying yourself an $80.00 dress. You are not suffering because you are denying yourself a brand-new car. If you are suffering, you are suffering because you have refused to deny yourself the pleasure of talking about your neighbor. If you are suffering, you are determined to sleep with another's husband or wife. If you are suffering, you have decided to get all you can get no matter who hurts. You will squash anyone that gets in your way. If you are suffering, it is because you have been a talebearer. You bring, and you carry gossip- far and near. If you are suffering, you are doing so because you are jealous of what another may have. If you are suffering, it is because you believe a lie rather than the truth.

Suffering is a result of your refusal to deny yourself. The word self- means that you believe all is wrapped up in you and you expect the world and everyone in it to bow to you. Self means that you believe you deserve that which you desire, and it is a privilege for people to give it to you. Self means that you have a right to get angry when things don't go your way. Self means that you give nothing but take everything. Self means that you have set yourself upon a pedestal. Self means that you have built an altar for yourself for people to sacrifice themselves to you. Not only themselves but all that they have and represent. Self means that if you feel like murdering someone, it is ok because you are somehow justified. Self means that if you decide to lie on another, you feel no compassion when doing it. Although you know that the lie could have someone thrown in jail or lose a job. Self says I have the right to think and do as I please. Self says, this is what I want, and I don't care how I get it, but I will have it. Self says, I will do what makes me look good even if it makes another appear evil.

You do not have to suffer.

Me: When I was growing up, the elders would say that they were suffering for Jesus. I have come to realize that this was a statement of perception and not of the truth.

Soul Source: *The truth is, Jesus suffered on the cross so you would not have to suffer. All the things in the world that would cause you to suffer, he bore on the cross. He came to set us free from suffering. He has made the way available. Now, all you have to do is choose the way he has made. Choose not to suffer by not allowing sin (self) to reign in your life. The choice you make will order your life. Your thoughts are a big part of this equation. The thoughts that you allow are the thoughts that will manifest in your life.*

To overcome suffering, bring every thought into captivity. Thoughts produce attitudes. Attitudes produce behavior. Behavior produces addiction and habit. Start thinking about what you think about. Order your thoughts to accomplish your purpose. Any thought that is against God, replace with a higher thought.

Insight 40

PROFIT VS. LOSING YOUR
SOUL

SOUL **Source:** *"What shall it profit a man if he gains the whole world and lose his soul. Or what shall a man give in exchange for his sole?"* When you lose your soul, you are not conscious anymore, nor do you care, about the things that will allow you to know God and have peace with your fellow man. You lose your mind and your thinking of such matters. When you lose your soul, you lose everything of the soul. Stay away from those things that will make you lose your soul. They are different for everyone. What makes one lose his soul may not make another do the same. What are these things for you?

Insight 41

LET THERE BE

S oul Source: *God gave Adam a directive in Chapter 1 of Gen-esis. God told Adam to be fruitful, multiply, and replenish the earth. He gave Noah those same instructions after the flood in Gen-esis 7. Although there is no record in the Bible as to the condition of the earth nor was there a description of the living things on the earth before the creation. However, since God told both Adam and Noah to replenish the earth, one would assume that the same kinds of life occupied the earth prior to the creation as it did after the creation and after the flood. One could assume this because of the definition of replenish- to reload; to renew; to restore; to restock.*

When he told these men to replenish the earth, it appears that he was telling them reproduce themselves many times over.

The Bible tells us that when the earth and the heavens were created in Genesis 1, the earth was void and without form and nothing existed except darkness and water. Then the Spirit of God moved upon the face of the waters. As he maneuvered upon the face of the deep, he used the word "let" over nine times in chapter one and each time the word "let" was used, a new part of the creation would appear. The word "let" means to permit; to allow; to authorize, and to consent to. If one were to take this definition at its face value, one could assume that creation was a result of permission and consent from God to the heavens and the earth to bring forth or reproduce or restore those things that were before but now were destroyed. In Genesis chapter 7, Noah, his family, and a pair of each animal were the only life saved after the flood. God this time however did not say, "Let" but rather he directed Noah to oversee the job of renewing and restocking the earth. This time Noah would supervise the replenishing of the earth for man and other living creatures. God made sure the condition of the earth was suitable for the renewing to take place.

In Genesis chapter 8:21-22, God told Noah that he would not curse the earth again for man's sake, but as long as the earth remained, seedtime and harvest, cold and heat, summer and Winter, and day and night shall not cease. When Adam fell in the Garden of Eden, God cursed the earth for his sake so that he would not have to curse man for yielding in the Garden. In Genesis 6:7,11,12,13, God repented that he made the living things upon the earth, including man. The Bible goes on to say in verses 11- 12 that the earth also was corrupt and filled with violence, for all flesh had corrupted his way upon the earth. Finally, in verse 13, God told Noah that he would destroy all flesh with the earth.

One could assume that when God cursed the earth, the earth then brought forth corruption. Being cursed, it brought the elements of that curse. The earth now was vexed, burdened, afflicted, and tributary. Like the creation story recorded in Genesis 1, the earth could only bring forth that which it possessed. Before the curse it brought forth life and light. Before the curse, the earth was not vexed or burdened. It freely gave of its substance abundantly to man. After

*the curse, it brought forth darkness and death. As the earth pro-
duced these things, Like Adam in the Garden of Eden, man gave
into and partook of the things in which the earth brought forth.
After the curse, the substance of the earth had to be earned by man.
The earth still had the good to offer along with the evil, but man
made a choice. By so doing, man himself became depraved, crooked,
dishonest, unscrupulous, fraudulent, degenerated, wicked, and con-
taminated just like the earth. Although God did not curse man,
man had a natural connection to the earth. Man was taken from
the earth and therefore was vulnerable and subject to the same behaviors of the earth if he gave expression to every thought and evil
imagination of his mind and heart. The Bible tells us that man's
thoughts and imagination were evil continually. Man reached a
point where he only thought about evil and therefore corrupted himself and added to the corruption of the earth. God in his mercy and
wisdom destroyed both man and the earth because the death of one
would only mean the same condition would eventually come to be
again. The destruction was a cleansing and purifying act. One
could better understand what Jesus meant when he said, "you cannot put new wine in an old bottle. The new wine would rend the
old battle, and both would be lost." God decided to start over.*

*When the earth was destroyed in Genesis chapter 7, the Bible records
that all living things died during the flood except the occupants of
the Ark. Verse 23 of chapter 7 tells one that every living substance
was also destroyed which was upon the face of the ground. The
word substance presents a very interesting thought when one ex-
amines its meaning. The word substance means essence; matter;
material; stuff; and property. If the very substance of the earth
was destroyed, one could reasonably think that "soulish" essence was
included as part of the extermination. In God's directive to Noah
to replenish the earth, could he also have been referring to restor-
ing the "soulish" condition or essence of the earth present before the*

corruption of the earth and man? Is it possible that when all the physical things were obliterated in the earth, all the "soulish" things also died? Could it be that the complete cleansing and destruction of the earth encompassed all the physical realities present at that time, all the "soulish" manifestation, and all expressed and unexpressed thoughts? If this is true, Noah not only oversaw replenishing life on earth, but it would also seem that he was responsible for replenishing honor, reverence, kindness, love, compassion, faith, beliefs, trust, righteousness, knowledge, understanding, thoughts, and the like.

This means that Noah had to live a conscious life; being always aware of what he was doing and why he was doing it. Noah had to guard his mind with diligence a corrupt thing would enter and defile him, and thereby defile the people on earth. Noah was to be the example of righteousness and other "soulish" elements in the earth. Noah's life was a measuring stick for all of his contemporaries. It was critical for Noah to think on those things that were true, honest, just, pure, lovely, virtuous, praiseworthy, and of a good report. His thoughts, when expressed and/or manifested, determined the direction and thought pattern of an entire world.

The flood and the blood of Jesus serve the same purpose - to rid man and the earth of corruption and death. Noah replenishes the earth after the flood in physical and "soulish" arenas. Jesus came to replenish the earth of right thoughts and right action. He came to restore the mind of God to man. He was anointed to preach good tidings unto the meek; he was sent to bind up the brokenhearted; to proclaim liberty to the captives, and the opening of prisons to them that are bound. He came so that man could have abundant life. He came to help man understand that they had dominion and that they are the sons of God. He came to tell them that they could do all things through Christ who strengthen them. He came to help them see the power God had bestowed upon them. He came to change man's thinking from death to life; from lack to abundance; from sin to righteousness; from hell to heaven; from need to desire; from man's way of thinking to God's way of thinking; from slave to sin to creator; and from killer to life giver.

Like Noah was the example to the people after the flood, Jesus is the example to all. Jesus said that we are to take his message to every corner of the world. He also said that greater things shall man do than he. Though Jesus stated in a different way than it was said in Genesis, the prime directive remains, "replenish the earth." If Jesus is our example, we are to replenish the earth with truth, righteousness, understanding, wisdom, and knowledge of God.

If we are successful in reaching every man, woman, and child with this message of the kingdom of God and if they accept and embrace the message, man will love God with all his heart, with all his soul, and with all his might. Treating his neighbor like himself will be second nature. Man's job is to live the message and share the message with others. "Be fruitful, multiply, and replenish the earth."

Insight 42

SEEK

SOUL **Source:** *Walk in thine own way and you meet with obstacles. Walk in the way of the Lord and you generate truth. Truth cometh not in the way you walk but the way you seek. Search out the way Jesus sought truth and follow his example.*

Truth is a microcosm of many things. It is here and there and gone tomorrow. Truth runs like a river stream- sometimes clear and other times muddy. The cleaner the water, the better you can see. When the truth is muddy, move to a clear place until you can see.

Truth is like a grizzly bear standing in front of you- you know that it is there.

Truth is never complicated but always simple.

Truth is like branches on a tree - it reaches in many directions.

Truth always comes at a price- that price is the loss of ignorance.

Truth rains down from heaven - forming shapes as it drops.

Truth can never be measured but always weighed.

Truth is a handshake. A gentlemen's agreement between two opposing forces.

Truth is distributive and reproductive.

Truth wins and everything else loses.

Truth is a shining star high in the heavens.

A search for truth is a search for wisdom.

Insight 43

LOVE THY NEIGHBOR

ME: Love thy neighbor as thyself is a well-known princi-ple taught by Jesus Christ. This would be an effortless thing to do. Apparently, people were having some problems with this concept and Jesus thought it worthy enough to be addressed by him.

Basically, people were then like they are today. They loved others as they loved themselves. They criticized themselves. "I am too fat." "I am too tall." "I cannot write good enough." "You are not pretty." Your feet are too big." They also criticize others. "You are too fat." "You are too tall." "You write good enough." "You are not pretty." Your feet are too big." They were involved in some destructive practices such as alcoholism, fornication, lying, stealing, jealousy, hatred, and anger. They encouraged others to engage in the same exercises or they would lie, steal, cheat, and hate others.

Soul Source: *The key to this principle of "love thy neighbor as thy-self" is to be sure you love yourself and then it becomes easy for you to love your neighbor in the same way.*

Man sees the world as he sees himself and interacts with the world accordingly. If he sees himself worthless, he will view others the same way and respond to them as such. He will criticize himself and criticize others. If he sees himself helpless, he will view others the same way and respond as such. He will complain about his condition and pity others for their condition. If he sees himself worthy, he will see others the same way and respond to others as such. He will see what is good about himself and will seek to do the same when interacting with others. If he is full of anger, he thinks others are angry and will usually find himself in conflict with others.

When you reach the point where you can see yourself like God sees you, you will love yourself. You will realize that God loves you no matter how tall you are, how short you are, how you look, how you speak, or how big your feet are. He is your creator, and he loves you just the way you are. There is nothing that you can do, say, or think that will ever separate you from the love of God.

Love begins with self- acceptance. When you accept yourself, you realize that you also can love yourself. Acceptance tells you that you do not have to be a certain size or look a certain way to be loved or approved of by God or others. If you think you do, others will sense this and begin to treat you as such. You are who you are and only you can tell others who you are. If you try to project a different image, you become a hypocrite and others will know this. When you are genuine, people will honor and respect you. You can live in the freedom of who you are when you are comfortable with allowing your real self to be revealed to the masses.

Allow love-to-love you and you will have no problem loving your neighbor. Love breeds' love. You can give what you have. If you have love, you will give love. In the end, the only thing that will remain is love. Do you love yourself?

Insight 44

ROBBING GOD

SOUL **Source:** *Can a man rob God? If a man can rob God, then man has robbed God of everything he has. God owns nothing and therefore you cannot rob him.*

God is a creator. Does a creator create that which is owned by others? God is different from the mythological gods. People worshipped and sacrificed them. I am neither to be worshipped nor sacrificed to. The Greek gods created nothing but owned and controlled everything. I created everything but own nothing. If I owned anything, there would be no freedom. You have freedom to operate in the way you were created. You cannot own that which you have created. Creator means to give.

Once you have created something, it takes on the personality of that which

you created it to be. From that point on, the thing or person is in charge of its own destiny. He cannot help but to be drawn to that which he was created to be.

God is the creator of the universe, but he owns nothing. Everything he created, he set free. How then can a man rob God? To rob God, God must own. If you desire something, you must go to the source.

To own that, which he creates, is to possess that which he never had. Everything that is used for creation comes from a particular source. Therefore, it belongs to someone else besides the creator. The heavens and earth were created from something that existed.

Me: Where did they come from?

Soul Source: *From another world.*

Me: You mean God is not an earthling?

Soul Source: *I mean man is not a universe. God comes from a world that is timeless and endless. The earth is only part of this world."*

God created Heaven and earth; it never said that God resided in heaven on earth. You think that heaven is on earth, and it is not.

I am the universe, and you live inside of me. I sustain you but I don't own you. That is why you will never be separated from me. Where you are, I am there because you live inside of me.

Everything in this universe is to be used by all creation as resources. All things belong to everybody. You can take possession of it for a time, but it is not yours.

The earth is a holographic projection. It is an illusion. It is your experience for this time.

You have to ask for what you desire. I have imbedded in everything the power to give you that which you request. I can tell you how to access what you desire. The only way to get your desires fulfilled is to ask the power source. The power source is not me but the thing in which I have granted the power to.

All things are made from substance and all substances have intelligence.

The creator takes something and makes something out of it.

Ownership does not necessarily imply possession. Ownership is explicit in responsibility. Are you not responsible for us? Not in the way you think. I have set all things in order to operate independent of me yet while they are dependent. They are dependent on me to give them what is needed to start life. Once life is started, they have everything at their disposal to sustain and shape life in any way they choose to do so. My responsibility to all is to give life-sustaining energies after that, they are own their own.

Me: I was always taught that you did all things.

Soul Source: *I do in a sense; in that I have placed all things in order and all things order themselves after the order I have placed upon them. I can reveal to anyone the order in which I have placed them. When you know the order, you know how to access what you desire.*

Opposites

Soul Source: *Only opposites exist. I created opposites. Just because a thing is opposite, does not make it bad. The opposite of man is woman. The opposite of up is down. The opposite of top is bottom. The opposite of left is right. The opposite of darkness is light. Each has its purpose, and each has its demands.*

All opposites are relative and personal. What is up to one may be down to another. What is male to one may be female to another. What is bottom to one may be top to another.

When you put a label on something, that is what it is for you. When you try to make it the same for everyone else that it is for you, that is sin. Good and evil only exist in the mind of man.

God created opposites out of what he knew about himself. God is love, so he created hate. Opposites were not created for man but for God. "All things were created by God and for God." The opposite of God is the only thing God is not.

Opposites help you to know and understand who God is and who he is not. Anything that is opposite of love, is not God. Man is the opposite of God, and he is the Son of God. That is why man can experience both worlds. God is only love and is able only to experience himself as love. God is only able to observe and participate in the opposite world created by him through man. So, in man is found the image of God and the opposite also of the image. Man is in a constant battle to subdue the opposite and experience God.

God experienced his opposite through Jesus Christ over 2000 years ago. That is why he understands man completely because he allowed himself to experience man completely. The only way man can experience God completely, is to allow himself to become God completely. As in heaven, let it be on earth. Heaven has already experienced earth. God desires man to experience the essence of his being. Man can only do this if his opposite part is annulated.

Insight 46

Faith

ME: I have read and heard about faith all my life. I never quite understood what it took to have faith. I was confused about how I could use faith to bring about things I wanted in my life. It seemed so easy for the people in the Bible to exercise their faith to do the things they wanted to do.

I now believe I have a clearer understanding of the scriptures. They now make sense to me. I will share my understanding of the scriptures and hope that it will help you clarify some things in your mind.

Me: Faith is the substance of things hoped for and the evidence of things unseen. Pay close attention to the word IS. My name is Regenia. My hair IS black and gray. A book IS something you read. The word IS is key in this scripture. Faith IS the substance of things hoped for. The word substance means material, essence, and stuff. Therefore, faith is the material, essence and stuff of things hoped for. If you hope for a car, faith is the essence, material, and stuff (substance) of a car.

All things are made of faith. There is nothing that is made or manifested that is not of faith. Therefore, that thing you hope for is made of faith.

Soul Source: *If you believe that all things are made of faith, you must know that good and bad things are made of faith, illness, disease, health, wealth, destruction, divorce, mental illness, etc. All things are made of faith. Whether consciously or unconsciously, we have now what we had faith for.*

Me: If faith is the substance of things hoped for, what do I need to do to manifest that for which, I hope?

Soul Source: *You simply know that the material, essence, and stuff (Substance or faith) of that which you hope for exist now. Faith IS and IS means exist and live. Since everything is made of faith, if it did not exist your faith would make it so. If you hope for money, know that money exists now. All you need to do is make it so for you. Know that the money that exists belongs to you. Do not concern yourself with where the money will come from, just know that it belongs to you. Knowing this will make it manifest in your life. Anything that is made of faith can be affected by faith. Anything that was put into place by faith, can be removed by faith, anything that can be removed by faith can be replaced by faith. If money and poverty came to you by faith, you can replace poverty by faith of abundance. Sickness can be replaced by faith in health. Low self-esteem can be replaced by faith in worth and value. Faith is the substance of things hoped for and the evidence of things not seen. The evidence of things not seen is the next discussion.*

Me: If faith is the substance of things hoped for and the evidence of things not seen," how does one get faith?

Soul Source: *Faith cometh by hearing and hearing by the word of God." Hearing brings faith (faith cometh by hearing). The meaning of the word hearing depends upon how it is being used.*

Me: Hearing what?

Soul Source*: Substitute the word hearing with knowledge.*

Me*:* Faith cometh by knowledge was something that I could understand. Not that I am contradicting the Bible, but I must make sense of the words so that I can apply them to my life. Faith cometh by knowledge stated a different way, is knowledge brings faith. If I hear (get the knowledge of) that they discovered a new planet, the knowledge of this brings faith that this happened or at least could happened. The more you hear the same thing, the more you will have faith that it really exists. If you hear that a woman had seventeen children, the knowledge of this would at least pique your interest that this did happen. If you hear it at least three times from three different sources (let the truth, be established by three or more witnesses), you more than likely would have faith that this is true. Let me be the first to tell you that my mother and father gave birth to seventeen children of which I am the seventh child. Faith cometh by hearing (knowledge) and hearing (knowledge) by the word of God. The last part of this verse, "hearing by the word of God," clarifies the issue of how and what you are to hear.

Soul Source: *"Hearing by the word of God," stated like "The word of God brings hearing (knowledge) helps you to see that hearing (knowledge) occur when the word of God is spoken or revealed. When you hear (get knowledge) of the word of God, faith cometh. When faith comes, it is the substance and evidence of that which you hear. When you hear (get knowledge) of the promises of God, faith* *comes and is the substance and evidence of the promises of God. All things are made of faith including the promises of God. You must claim the promises of God as your own to make them so for you. You must know that the promises of God exist now and are alive.*

Me: How does faith work?

Soul Source: *Faith worketh by love. Stated in another way, love makes faith work. To understand how you get faith and how you make faith work for you are two different things. Without love faith cannot work. Without love for that which you hear (get knowledge of) or that which you have faith (substance) of, faith cannot bring about those things. Remember love has spaces and when dealing with faith, those spaces must be filled with the faith (substance, material, stuff, essence) of that which you hope for and that which you hear (get knowledge of).*

If God promises you health, you must have a love for health and fill the spaces of love regarding health with health consciousness. Your love for health will motivate you to think, live, and sleep healthily. If you hope for money, your love for money will encourage you to think about money, see money, and sleep money. Your love for being the best in your profession will cause you to think, meditate, and plan. If you love anything, your love for a thing will cause you to fill the spaces of love with that thing. If you love the word of God, you will think, sleep, and meditate upon the word of God constantly. Love causes consistency of action.

You can fill your love spaces with anything you want if you have met the conditions of love. If you fill your spaces for any other reasons, it will not manifest because it is not of love, it is of lust. Lust is when you want it to heap upon yourself. Faith worketh by love.

Do not confuse love with possession. Possession means that you own a thing or person. Love says you care enough about a person or thing to give all that you have without expecting anything in return.

Love fills the spaces because love has a desire to be intimate with a person or thing. Love wants to share itself with that person or thing.

Love will not be hurt if the person or thing does not do likewise. Possession gets upset and angry if the person or thing does not return its affection. If a man says he loves a woman and thinks of her all the time. He may call it love but the young lady may call it possession since the young man gets angry when she does not return what he thinks as reciprocal affection.

Love understands that there may not be a reciprocal act but chooses to fill the spaces with the thing or person it loves regardless.

Insight 47

EVERYONE IS LOOKING FOR
THE SAME THING

ME: I believe God created the family so that everyone would have someone to talk with, be comforted by, protected, and to simply care about.

When you feel like the only time you hear from a family member is when they need something, you become very disheartened, angry, and somehow feel abused and taken advantage of. I was feeling just this way one Sunday afternoon after receiving a phone call from a member of my family. She wanted some money to take care of a bill. I suppose one would be a little more enthusiastic about a call for help if an occasional call to inquire about your welfare were made. Granted, I have always felt obligated to provide what I can to my family members whenever they needed something. When I could not do it, I felt guilty.

I am from a very large family. Except for a few family members, the only time I hear from my family is when they want or need something. It seemed that my importance to them is directly proportionate to how much I can give. Don't get me wrong, I love to give and desire always to be a blessing to others. But everyone wants to feel cared about without strings.

This Sunday afternoon, it seemed that I was a bit upset than usual and wanted some space and time to figure out how I was to think about my family and how was I to respond. There is a little garden in Rock Hill called Glencairn Garden. My husband and I used to frequent this place many years ago. We loved it for its peaceful surroundings and serene setting. This garden has beautiful trees, and the variety of the flowers and shrubs are incredible. In the middle of the garden is a tri level fountain that empties into a pond filled with fish and water lilies. In the spring, the Azaleas are breathtaking. All colors, shapes, and varieties. There are paved and unpaved walking trails among tall trees. The small bridges allow you an opportunity to stop and watch the flow of the water or take notice of the frogs and other small aquatic animals do whatever they do. The wildlife played undisturbed by your presence. I had to find just the right spot for this talk with God. I walked until I spotted a bench on the south side of the fountain under a tall oak tree. There I sat and began to cry.

I was upset that usually this person called when she needed something. But I was also struggling with feeling abused and used given this person's relations to me. How could I possibly feel this way? I also debated my loyalty and being in line with the word of God. I conflicted with my own thoughts and feelings. I was feeling sorry for myself and started bashing this person and others for putting me in a position where I was questioning me. Then I heard it

Soul Source: *Everyone is looking for the same thing.*

Me: I understood perfectly what he was saying. There are times when we look for things in other people. But those people are looking for the same thing in you or in someone else. What you need or want may not always come from the same person you provide like things. For example, money may not come from the same person you give money. Gifts may not come from the same person you give gifts to. If a person does not give you what you are looking for, it just means that they don't have it for you. If you admire someone, that person may or may not have admiration for you. If you are looking for comfort from a person, she may not have it to give to you but may provide it to another whom she sees would benefit from it. Everyone is looking for the same thing. Everyone is looking for love. Each of us has our own ideas of love and how an individual can express that best. A mother may decide that her son can show her love by supporting her. A father may decide that a daughter can express her love best by cooking for him or caring for him in his old age. If the son or the daughter does not express love in this manner, the mother and father may feel unloved and unappreciated. The son and daughter, however, may be doing several other loving things because it is what they have to give to them.

Everyone is looking for the same thing. Everyone is looking for understanding, truth, justice, faith, trust, patience, and security, etc. Since everyone is looking for the same thing, don't be disappointed if you don't find what you are looking for in an individual. This individual may be looking for the same thing from you. If he is looking for you to give it to him, he cannot give you what he is looking for from you.

Soul Source: *We all must learn to receive that which is given us by everyone, and we will always have what you are looking for from someone.*

Me: A person may not give you what you want them to give, but they have something to give to you. What you are looking for will not necessarily be found in the person you want it to be found in. That person may or may not have it to give or simply does not want to give that thing to you.

When this family member calls to make a request of me, she gives me her confidence that I could do it. On the other hand, she may not call another family member for money but may call them to discuss personal problems. For whatever reason, our relationship has evolved to this point, and I suppose I had something to do with how our relationship is shaped. If I don't like it, then I will have to change it.

Soul Source: *Remember, everyone is looking for the same thing.*

Be careful when you get angry and upset at others when they do not provide what you think they should provide. Everyone is looking for the same thing. When you say they should give you what you are looking for, you are making a law that they cannot keep. Even if a person is able to obey your shoulds for a while, soon or later, they will break your law that will result in anger and frustration. Allow others to also live under grace. You may not always be able to provide what people are looking for, but don't get angry if they ask. You too are looking for the same thing from God, yourself, or others.

WHY MUST THERE ALWAYS BE A REASON?

ME: Each morning, I listen to ministers on TV as I prepare to go to work. I have attended church since I was a small child. I have been a participant of several religious services. I have been in the company of men and women whom I considered called and anointed by God to preach and teach his word. I have attended meetings of prophets and Apostles and attended meetings of healers and teachers. I have sat in the company of elders who have been members of their church for decades. I have gone to hear well-known men and women of faith. More than 98% of what I hear from the elders, prophets, teachers, preachers, apostles, and leaders are that there is a reason you do not receive what God has promised in his word.

Last week I listened as a preacher passionately taught that the reason that you do not receive the promises of God was because you are disobedient. I also heard a preacher preach that the reason you do not receive is that you did not meditate on his word. I heard another preacher talk about the reason you do not receive is because you do not give. Yet another preacher expounds on the fact that the reason you do not receive the promises of God is because you do not love one another. Someone of the other reasons for not receiving the promise of God is:

- You do not tithe

- You do not pray

- You do not read his word

- You do not have a personal relationship with Jesus

- You are not mature

- You are carnal minded

- You do not walk with understanding

- You do not know God

- You do not know how to apply his word

- You do not pray right

- You are high minded

I have spent a great deal of time trying to do a number of these things that the teachers and preachers told me I must do to receive the promises of God. Yet, I find myself still wondering why I do not enjoy the full range of blessings that my heavenly

Father promised me. The reason that some may give is that I have not made a deep commitment and therefore I have not received. Another may say that I have to wait patiently for the Lord. But I contest these notions. If God has promised me, why must I do or why must I wait?

Some may say you must do so because his promises are conditional. For each promise of prosperity, there is a condition to receiving it. But what is the condition? Is the condition from God or is the condition from man? The law is unconditional, grace is divine. The spirit has no conditions.

When I listen to the teachers and the preachers and hear all the things I must do before I can receive the promises, I could get quite discouraged. It seems to be that by the time I get one thing right, there will always be another reason given for not receiving the promises of God. This philosophy is built on works and not faith.

The next time you hear you are not receiving the promises, just remember, faith and obedience are the only things that matter.

Soul Source: *Faith and obedience are not reasons because they are spiritual. Anything spiritual has no reason. Anything that has to do with the law gives a reason.*

Insight 49

BEING IN AWE

SOUL **Source:** *Being in awe about people and things of the world blocks you from being in awe of God. If the world captivates you, you pledge your allegiance to the world because that is what you focus on. Part of "setting the captives free" is to help them see that awe captivates.*

Being in awe captives your attention, your allegiance, your loyalty, your creative abilities, and everything within you is devoted to pleasing the people and going after things which you are in awe of.

You are in awe of gold, nice cars, fine clothing, lavish foods, mansions, etc. Anything we do not have but desire, we stand in awe of those things. The awe-ness encourages you to seek them.

Me: Could this be what is meant by "Seek ye first the Kingdom of God and these things will be added on?"

Soul Source*: We stand in awe of one's position and one's possession. You stand in awe of slender bodies, so we spend millions of dollars on diet aids. We stand in awe of black hair; so, we spend billions of* *dollars on something called dye. You stand in awe of automobiles, so we spend the best years of our life working to pay for something you only ride in an average of two hours per day. The rest of the time you are working or resting.*

When you stand in awe, it disrupts your thinking and you often become afraid and intimidated. When Satan took Jesus up on the mountain and offered him everything, he was betting that Jesus would be in awe of all Satan was offering him: the power, glitter, prestige, honor, and glory. But Jesus responded, "It is written." Jesus was clearly saying that he was not in awe of those things and therefore they did not have captivating power over him. If they could not capture him, they could not have power and authority over him.

You should not be in awe of anyone and should not want anyone to be in awe of you. No matter what you do, you do not deserve awe. Awe is reserved for the one who is awe.

The spirit is named "capture" and "bondage" and everything else that goes along with these things: lying, stealing, dishonesty, deception, etc. Hadn't you heard of a person so captivated by money that he steals for it, lies for it, hurt people for it, and kills for it?

The only thing that deserves awe is AWE himself. The thing demands itself. Therefore, only AWE can demand awe. The Israelites built a golden calf and were in awe of it. They were in awe of some thing that was not awe. They were in awe of something that was made by awe. They began to corrupt themselves and to commit all manner of evil within their camp. When you are in awe, you will corrupt yourself with all manner of things you do not want to do.

The Israelites were in awe of the giants in the land and that brought about fear. Awe of anything often brings about fear. If you are in awe of a judge in a court of law, you will not be able to speak as you should because you are afraid of the judge. If you are in the presence of a famous person, you will not be able to speak with him the way you want to if you assign her awe. Anyone you hold in awe; you will assign awe to him or her.

Me: When people visit the cities around America, they are easily identified as tourists because they are pointing, taking pictures, looking up, and staring. That is why you hear reports of tourists being robbed. At the moment you are in awe, you are captives.

Soul Source. *Save your assignment of awe to awe him, God and you will never have to care about being a captive. When you assign awe to something other than God, you are actually robbing God and giving it to something made by God. Robbing means you take it without permission. He will never give his permission for awe to be assigned to something other than him. If he allows awe to be taken away, he allows his essence to be taken from him. If he does not have an essence, then he cannot exist in the same form he exists now.*

Get rid of the awe you hold for people and things, and you get rid of many bondages and captivity.

Insight 50

A GIFT

ME: How do you know when something is a gift? As my husband and I were returning from a business trip, we were discussing many interesting issues. We were trying to solve the problems of the world and family. Our discussion led us to explore the meaning of a gift and how do you know when you have received a gift.

My husband said, "I believe anything that God gives to you that you must share it with other people." "If you don't, then God is not pleased because he gives it to you to benefit others as well as benefit yourself." When he said that, it was like a light bulb went off in my head.

Soul Source: *A gift it is something that must be beneficial to you otherwise it is not a gift at all."*

Many things we call gifts are not gifts at all but rather our own creation that we have labeled gift. A true gift means that it was something given without cost to you.

Insight 51

JUSTICE

Me: Everyone is crying out for justice. But where and who are "the just"?

Soul Source: *The just shall live by faith. Only "the just" can demand justice. Unjust men are void of justice. Therefore, they cannot demand, nor do they understand justice.*

Me: I thought everyone understood what justice is. Are you telling me that everyone does not understand justice?

Soul Source: *I am telling you that "the just" shall live by faith. If there is no faith, there can be no justice. That which a person has faith in is the thing that justifies him. The just has faith in God. Those who put their faith in other things besides God are unjust. That which they have faith in justifies everything they do and think. Justified, justice means being right with or in agreement with that you have placed your trust in.*

Being just and doing justice are two different things. Being just means you have agreed with God that what he says is right. Doing justice means you do what God tells you to do.

Me: What is justice?

Soul Source: *Depends on whom you ask. To a child, justice is getting its own way. To a mother, justice is protecting her children. To a father, justice is being able to provide for the family. To a preacher, justice is having his congregation follow him. To a teacher, justice is being able to teach without interference. To a judge, justice is upholding the law. To a buyer, justice is getting the best for the lowest price. To a seller, justice is getting the highest price possible. To a student, justice is getting the* grade earned without regard to race.

Me: What about to God? What is justice to God?

Soul Source: *Justice to God is plain and simple; wait on the Lord.*

Me: What do you mean? How can waiting on the Lord be justice?

Soul Source: *Waiting on the Lord is justice because it allows God to bring forth that in your life that needs to be brought forth. Justice to me is an unfoldment of one's ego and one's truth. Justice is times past, present, and future; is always the same, bring it to God and leave it there. Remember, "The just shall live by faith."*

To do justice is to set the captives free. Justice is about equality. God is not a respecter of person. He is just. You are a woman of laws and judge others by your laws. I am just according to me not to you. If you labor under the law, some things you see on this earth will grieve you. "Be of good cheer for I have overcome the world." Your job is to believe that I have set things straight in the hearts of men and you must behave like you believe that I have done this thing.

It is a law when it brings great depression, sadness, hopelessness, and judgment. The law kills. There is no life in the law. "Where the spirit of the Lord is, there is liberty."

Me: If there was no law from Adam to Moses, what was it?

Soul Source: *Grace! He freed me from laws.*

Insight 52

THE POWER OF AGREEMENT

A GREEMENT (noun): compromise, compact, accord, harmony, arrangement, understanding, and pact. Agree (verb): acknowledge, admit, concede, recognize, allow, assent, coincide, harmonize, accord, conform, correspond, and fit.

Me: How you can help others think better of themselves, was the discussion of my Sunday school class on a cold and windy Sunday morning. It occurred as I sat listening to the discussion that I hadn't the faintest idea how to make one think well about oneself. But how could I not know. After all, I worked with children for twenty-five years who had low self-esteem as a constant companion.

I heard this question raised hundreds of times to people of diverse backgrounds and cultures. I guess most were listening to the same person because the response to the question of "how to help someone think better of himself" was "tell them that they are somebody." I remember being in the classroom with students who thought of themselves as nobody. No matter how many times we tried to encourage them, they just could not seem to shake themselves loose from these thoughts. What I did not realize then, and not until that very moment sitting in a Sunday school class, was that there were so many things in their environment that reinforced their belief of who they were.

Who they were in their own eyes were children who were helpless, dumb, in need of special assistance, poor, and isolated. Indeed, the school they were attending was a school only for students with intellectual disabilities. At Christmas time and on other holidays, the community brought them food and clothing. Not only did I encourage this, but also in many instances, I arranged and solicited help from community agencies for them. They were in a school with only special education teachers and special support staff. They were reading materials written for first and second grade students. They were provided with free lunch, and any other special accommodation that was supposed to enable them to achieve.

On the surface there was nothing wrong with trying to help those who we perceive could help themselves. I said on the surface. Did we really help those children? I see some of those students from time to time, and they are no better off than they were then. In fact, they are probably worse off because of age, responsibility, and no skills to help them maneuver successfully in this world. Now I see the part I played in helping them sustain such a world that is filled with disappointment and pain.

I also think about the housing projects, thrift stores, and soup kitchens. I think about the sick in hospitals across this country. My thoughts are drawn to my father and the years he spent in pain and suffering and to my sister who died a young woman because lupus destroyed her organs. I think about the young people who believe that they do not deserve better than they have right now. I think about the kids who struggle in the home with parents who are drug addicts and the only thing that they understand is that they are doomed to a life of misery and despair.

I think about all these things and my mind wonders to the Bible where Jesus in Matthew 18:18-19, "Verily I say unto you, whatsoever ye shall bind on earth it shall be bind in heaven whatsoever you loose on earth, it shall be loosed in heaven." "Again, I say unto you, that if two of you shall agree on earth as touching anything that they shall ask, it shall be done for them of my Father which is in heaven."

When we agree with someone, we are asking that the Father grant it since the Father has all power to grant that which we ask. By agreeing with someone here on earth, God will allow it to be so. He will never overturn our will. When you do not agree with someone on earth, you are asking the father not to grant this thing because you do not agree with it.

But a person has free will. Just because you do not agree with what they are asking does not mean they cannot or will not find someone to agree with them. For if a person says that he is poor and you respond by saying, no you are rich. He will think that you are crazy and obviously cannot see his clothing or living conditions. So that person will continue to search for someone who agrees with him. When he finds someone to agree with him, his petition is granted. If he wants to continue his state in life, all he must do is to always surround him with those who agree with his assessment of his life. Drunkards surround themselves with drunkards. Thieves surround themselves with thieves. Liars surround themselves with liars. Crooks surround themselves with crooks. Poor people surround themselves with poor people. No matter who it is, a person is always looking for a partner to agree with their existence.

The partner poor people found to agree with them was the welfare system. When the government decided to reform welfare, all they were saying was "I am not going to agree with you anymore." I am not going to agree that you have too many children to work. I am not going to agree with you that you cannot support yourself and your family. I am not going to agree with you that a lack of education prevents you from getting a job. I am not going to agree with you that you are lazy. I am not going to agree with you that you have no dignity or pride. At the same time, they said, "I believe you can earn a living, hold a decent paying job, get your dignity and respect back, and you will find decent and affordable childcare. Because I believe you can do these things, I will help you by providing opportunities, but you will have to take advantage of them. Those welfare recipients who agreed with the government's new position and policy regarding welfare reform are now earning money and holding a decent paying job. Those who did not agree with the government are still trying to find another person or organization to agree with them that they are poor and cannot help themselves.

People who are overweight and have convinced themselves that they cannot control their eating unless they have some help, find their partner in companies who produce diet aids and foods. It is amazing the amount of money Americans spend on diet aid and products. Overweight people say that they cannot control their appetite and the diet companies say you are correct. As long as overweight people agree with the diet companies and the diet companies agree with the overweight people, both will have a long loving relationship. **Amos 3:3** "Can two walks together, except they be agreed." We agree on many aspects of our lives.

- Partnership

- Contract (i.e., job, house, car, clothes)

For an agreement to take place, there must be at least two parties involved.

- You and your supervisor: Why do most people get fired?

- Student and teacher: Conflict

- Father and son: conflict

- Mother and daughter: conflicts

We agree with other people about ourselves.

- **Physical Appearance.** For some of you, people have told you, you are handsome or pretty. The first few times you kind of fluff it off. But after the fifth or the sixth time, you start believing it.

- Wardrobe

- Personality - nice person, quiet,

- Intelligence (IQ test, SAT/ACT test)

We agree with other people about other people.

- Sometimes we agree with what the news media say about people. We allow the news media to tell us what we should like and dislike; who is pretty or handsome; who is great and who is not also great; talented and who is not; who is right and who is wrong.

- Sometimes we agree with what our friend has to say about another person.

- Sometimes we agree with our co-workers about the supervisor. Sometimes we agree with others about the minister of pastor of the church.

We agree with other people about the state of the world.

- The world is sure in a mess

- I don't know what we are going to do with generation X. It is a lost generation.

- You can't trust anybody

- Everybody is out to get what they can

- The weather is crazy and unpredictable

- We will never have peace in certain parts of the world

We agree with others about their state in the world

- A Black man can never get ahead because those white folks are keeping them down

- All I can do is make ends meet

- Every time I make a dollar, I have to spend ten

- If it isn't one thing is another

- I could never live in a $200,000 home

- I can only afford Bojangles

- I want to shop on Fifth Avenue, but I know I can't. There is nothing wrong with shopping at K-mart.

- I am poor and need some help. (Xmas and Thanksgiving baskets)

We want others to agree with us about our state (how we perceive our state) in the world

- Shoulder and neck pain (tell story)

- I have no money to buy a fancy car

- I am sick

- I am poor

- I am overworked

- I need help

- I can hardly make it

- I tried; but I can't

Some reason I do not understand, it seems as though we seek out someone to agree with us when it is negative. For example, I don't hear too many people going around and saying:

- I am a king and priest

- I am the head and not the tail

- I am royalty

- I am beautiful

- I am wise

- I am smart

- I am a great dancer

- I am a great writer

- I am a wonderful mathematician

- I am a great basketball player

- I am a good singer

- I have a great figure

- I am rich

- I am healthy

- I am happy

- I have joy

- I have peace

Agreement is powerful because it means that you give your consent to whatever is at hand. Good or bad; right or wrong; helpful or hurtful. Every response is an answer to a question. Questions and answers govern the world and the universe. Like anything else, power of agreement, this servant (because that is what the act of agreement is- a servant) can be used to make life fruitful or destroy life.

If others agree with you that you are

- Sick

- Poor

- Helpless

- Sinner saved by grace

- Can't measure up

- Only a "D" student

Your focus should be on getting others to agree with you that you are:

- Smart

- Beautiful

- Handsome

- Intelligent

- Are a god

- Prince

- Wise

- Live forever

- You can do anything through Christ which strengthens you

Soul Source: *People will look at you like you crazy at first, but if you keep saying these things, they will come around. Just like you came around when someone first told you that the dress you thought was ugly really looks pretty good on you.*

Just think about this for a moment. If you can find just one person to agree with you that you are healthy, wealthy, and wise, what that would mean to you? If you can find one person to stay in agreement with you so that you will know who you are and what you have been sent to earth to do, you indeed would experience something that most people do not.

Agreements can be made with one person, a group, an organization, or with a country.

Me: Throughout the Bible, you will find where people made agreement and the significance of that agreement.

- David agreed with the prophet Samuel that he was King

- Mary agreed with the Angel that she would be the Mother of the savior

- The disciples agreed that they would be fisher of men

- Jesus agreed with God that he would be the savior

- Moses agreed with God that he would lead the people out of bondage

- Joshua agreed with God that he would lead the people into the promise land

- Solomon agreed with God that he was wiser or richer than anyone before him or after him

- The Holy spirit agreed with God that he would be our comforter

Insight 53

What Is Man Saved From?

ME: What is man saved from and what does the blood of Jesus has to do with it?

Soul Source: *First let's examine your first question. What is man saved from? Man is not saved from anything but rather he is brought to something. He is brought to knowledge and understanding and wisdom. The church has said that you are saved but I say that you are brought to knowledge, wisdom, and understanding. In that way, I guess you could say that man is saved from and unknowing fate. Without knowledge, wisdom and understanding, he can never find his way back home. He would live this lifetime as a citizen of the world. When he is brought to knowledge. Wisdom, and understanding, he views himself as being in a strange land and a sojourner.*

Me: What knowledge is he brought to?

Soul Source: *All knowledge. First, he is brought to the knowledge that he does not know. Then he is brought to the knowledge that he can know. Then he is brought to the knowledge that he must know. Then to the knowledge of what he must know.*

Me: What knowledge is he brought to?

Soul Source: *That I am the way, truth, and life and none come to the father but by me.*

Me: Does that mean that I cannot converse with the Father?

Soul Source: *It means that there is a process by which you converse.*

Me: What do you mean?

Soul Source: *Three phases – follow the example: The truth, the way, and the life.*

Me: What is life?

Soul Source: *Life is an understanding. You structure life according to what you understand. Life is creative. Life is not high or low, peaks or valleys. Life is the essence of these things but not these things. Life captures the moments. That moment that you cannot remember loses life. Life is always an awakening. Life is experiencing. Life resists or rejects nothing but embraces everything. Death is life dead. No one can define life because it is an experience evolving with the individual. Life takes nothing but give relentlessly. The nature of life is to give.*

What Does It Profit A Man?

Soul Source: *What does it profit a man if he gains the whole world and lose his very soul? Or what would a man give in exchange for his soul?*

What does it profit a man if he gains the admiration of others and loses his identity?

What does it profit a woman if she is honored for accomplishment and has not achieved true joy?

What does it profit a man if he gains riches but have guilt and regret about how he came to be rich?

What does it profit a woman if she gains a big house but is in debt and debt is bondage?

What does it profit a man if he gains a nice car but have to make car payments?

What does it profit a woman if she gains a beautiful wardrobe but pay on a credit card each month?

What does it profit a man if he gains fame and lose his way to Christ?

What does if profit a woman if she gains unfathomable knowledge abuts loses wisdom?

What does it profit a woman if she gains pride but loses compassion?

What does it profit a man if he is fearful but cannot or will not exercise courage?

What does it profit a woman if she gains tremendous wealth but hoards it?

What does it profit a man if he harbors unforgiveness and never lives in the state of forgiveness?

What does it profit a woman if she dwells on death but refuses to live in the moment?

What does it profit a man if he has understanding but acts like a fool?

Insight 55

Freedom and life

Soul **Source:** *Life starts with freedom. The freedom of life. The freedom of all. The freedom to taste. The freedom to see. The freedom to understand. The freedom to seek. The freedom to fly. The freedom to whine. The freedom to be.*

Get rid of all the rules. Rules binds: don't do this and don't do that will eventually kill you. You die long before death. Rules will make it so. Live without rules and you will live a fruitful life.

Live by your heart. By attention to your feelings. Never do or say anything because that is what the rule of someone has said or done. Life by your own code.

Me: We raise our children by codes and rules, is that wrong?

Soul Source: *Nothing is wrong, but you will turn out other people who are bound and therefore unhappy because they want to do something contrary to your rules.*

Me: Should you let children do what they want?"

Soul Source: *Yes, exactly what they want.*

Me: Sometimes what they want to do will harm them.

Soul Source: *Yes, but that too is what they want and eventually they will have it.*

Soul Source: *The life you see that is tied in struggle is a life waiting to be free. Freedom eluded them because they refused to look at their circumstances and their human condition. They denied that they were freed but rather focused on the time when they would be free.*

There are different degrees of life – sparse to abundance." "Abundant life is a state of mind and being.

You asked and you shall receive. Abundant life is a spiritual awakening to the essence of life – that which is the life blood of life.

Soul Source: *What is the essence of life?" "It is not a thing but a place you get to when you fully recognize who you are and who God is in you. Without God, life force (essence), there is no life.*

What Is Good

Soul **Sources:** *For it is written all is good that is good that which is no good is not good. It was not made good and will never be good. Stop trying to make good out of evil. In evil there is not good. Now will there ever be good.*

Look back at those things that God made and call them good. Them and only them are good. All other things that are made are not good. Only the purest form is good.

Read the creation story, which is where you will find all that is good because all was made by the hands of God." Do you understand?

Me: Why the lesson on good?

Soul Sources: *You need to know what is good at this time in your life to keep you from evil. Remember good always and honor me by choosing the good.*

Light is good. God divided the darkness from the light. Darkness is not good. Good is called forth or permitted. A division is necessary for the good to show forth. Good and evil cannot co-exist. Something is necessary to support or sustain good.

Earth and seas are good.

Reproduction is good. Everything of its own kind.

Two great lights are good. The greater to rule over the earth by day and the lesser by night.

Water creatures and winged fowl bring forth after its kind.

Beast, cattle, creeping thing after its kind is good. Permitting that which is innate and then duplicating it.

Man is good.

FAITH AND LOVE

Soul Sources: *When love and fear separate, it takes time to replace that fear with faith. Love worketh by faith. When you have more faith in you, in time, you will have faith in others. The faith you have in yourself and the faith you have in others is different, yet the same. You have faith in your abilities, strengths, beliefs, etc. The faith you have in others must be one that confirms your belief that they can increase their faith in themselves. That is what I (God) mean when I (God) say your faith will spread to others. When others see the faith, you have in yourself, they will understand the power of that and will seek faith in themselves.*

Strive to help others evaluate faith in themselves because then and only then, can they love themselves because "love worketh by faith." In the absence of faith, there is no love. It is important that the faith you have in someone is not of the faith that they can do something for you but is of the faith that they can do for themselves. Helping them to increase faith in themselves helps them to love. People love you when they try to help you love yourself.

Reject the faith someone has in you to perform a task for them. Anyone who performs a task without loving the task has no faith and without faith, all shall come to an end. Maybe that is the secret to why some things last longer than others. Faith gives life and life sustains it.

If someone says, "I love you" and has no faith that you are or can develop you, they do not love you, but they love what they think you can do for them.

Faith also provides freedom. If you have faith that a person has faith, you will let them fly. If you fear that they be afraid of themselves, you will keep them shut up. Love leaves when you stop believing in a person's ability to get him/herself together. You think they will never see the light. But if you retain the faith that they will see the light God wants them to see, you can begin to love again. However, this time your love will propel them inward and upward, rather than outward.

I (God) am you and you are I. When you have faith in yourself, you will have faith in me.

MATHEMATICS ANSWERS EVERYTHING

From What Source Did This Come?

One night in March 2006, I remember suddenly waking up with this thought clearly imprinted on my mind.

Soul Source: *Mathematics answers all things.*

Me: Deep sleep or partially awake when the thought materialized, I cannot tell. I contemplated the thought on the edge of my bed for a few minutes. Then I laid back down and drifted off to sleep.

In the days following, I brought the subject up with my husband and colleagues. As weeks passed, I found myself sharing it with anyone willing to engage. It seemed I was seeking validation, eager to ascertain the rationality of my thoughts. Subsequently, I penned my reflections on this matter in this book, referring to it now as a hypothesis. It remains unverified and speculative, and I have no intention of pursuing empirical validation. Instead, I anticipate that time and circumstances will either affirm or refute it.

I encapsulate this idea under the title "Mathematics Answers Everything," a revelation that dawned on me in an almost prophetic manner. Each day unfolds more of its relevance in my life, manifesting in a multitude of interactions with others. It's become clear that the hypothesis harbors unique consequences for different individuals and scenarios.

The more we attune ourselves to the mathematical aspects of existence, the more we can influence our destinies. Mathematics pervades every facet of life, an undeniable truth we can either choose to engage with actively or passively endure its outcomes.

Mathematics transcends disciplines, harboring no biases or motives. It remains indifferent to distinctions of race, religion, gender, or economic status. Its impact is inevitable, touching everyone in varied ways. At its core, mathematics deals with sums, calculations, and predictions, allowing us to forecast the behaviors and beliefs that emerge under certain conditions and environments. By altering these variables, we have the power to modify the mathematical outcomes in our lives, thus reshaping our beliefs and behaviors.

About the Author

Regenia Mitchum Rawlinson, celebrated author of eleven books, fervently champions life's enrichment through the cultivation of inner strength, steadfastly relying on the boundless power within us. She ardently advocates for uplifting one's existence by tapping into this innate reservoir of strength, firmly believing in the inherent potential within each individual.

Alongside her husband, David, they reside in South Carolina, finding fulfillment in their roles as parents to three adult children and embracing the joys of grandparenthood.

Milton Keynes UK
Ingram Content Group UK Ltd.
UKHW012321290524
443431UK00001B/16